A RACING CAR DRIVER'S WORLD

Rudolf Caracciola

A RACING CAR

DRIVER'S

WORLD

FARRAR, STRAUS AND CUDAHY
NEW YORK

Translated from the German by Sigrid Rock

Published simultaneously in Canada by Ambassador Books, Ltd.,
Toronto. Manufactured in the United States of America. Published
in Germany under the title Meine Welt *by Limes Verlag, Wiesbaden.*
The quotation from The Kings of the Road *is used with the permission*
of Mr. Ken Purdy.

Of those on the Mercedes team,
Rudolf Caracciola was the best. . . .

—Ken Purdy,
The Kings of the Road

A RACING CAR DRIVER'S WORLD

1

I believe that every man can achieve the goal he strives for. I also believe that every man who feels in himself a strong desire to do a certain job will eventually end up doing that job, no matter how many detours he has to take to get there.

I wanted to become a racing driver from my fourteenth birthday on. My wish seemed a hopeless one. In the middle-class circles in which I was raised, automobile racing was considered the passion of mad, rich people or a special kind of eccentricity, like tightrope walking for instance.

My father wanted to send me to a university. This plan collapsed when it became evident that the contents of the books could not be brought into harmony with the contents of my head. So with a high school diploma I left school forever.

Shortly afterward my father died. The family council got together and decided that I should find a good hotel somewhere, learn the hotel business from the ground up, and, once I was trained, work in my father's hotel on the Rhine. Family members make for cheap labor.

But I wanted to become a racing driver.

Finally a compromise was made. I was sent, as an apprentice, to work in an automobile factory, Fafnir's, in Aachen. Probably this strange indulgence on the part of the family council was based on their assumption that the grimy work in a factory would spoil my appetite for automobiles forever and send me back ruefully to the clean-scrubbed family hearth.

However, it turned out differently. I remained in the factory for over a year. And if something hadn't happened that forced me to leave my job abruptly and under cover of night, I'd probably have stayed on, because I didn't dislike the work. My fellow mechanics were honest, straightforward fellows without a false streak in them and I got along fine with all of them.

One evening three of us went to the Kakadu, a night club, with the fiancée of one of them, Karl Kruppke. Kruppke's girl wanted to see some of the night life of Aachen. The Kakadu was jammed, and it was so noisy you couldn't hear yourself think. The people sat crammed together and perspiring waiters were pushing their way among them.

We found seats in a red leather upholstered booth. At the end of the long, narrow restaurant was a dance floor where a band was playing. You could see the musicians move but only rarely did a few notes from the piano or a wail from the saxophone penetrate through the crowd to us. It was as if the band played behind a glass wall.

The waiter came and we ordered three brandy and sodas and for the girl a vermouth soda, the cheapest drinks on the menu. Kruppke got up and danced with his fiancée. He was a gnarled little fellow with bowlegs. He looked like a friendly leprechaun. She was half a head taller than he. When the dance was over and they returned to our table, the girl looked very pretty with her flushed face under the ash-blond hair.

In the booth across from us sat three officers of the occupation army. When the next dance began, one of them came over to our table. He was a tall, skinny Belgian lieutenant with a small black mustache and a face that was pale except for a fiery red scar on his forehead, which looked like a saber wound.

"Excuse me, monsieur," he murmured, bowing to Kruppke.

Kruppke stared at him but said nothing. The officer bowed to the girl. She put down her little red patent leather bag, ran her hand over her hair, and was about to get up. At that instant Kruppke said in a rough voice:

"No!" And again, even more loudly: "No!"

The Belgian turned around. Kruppke rose slowly to his feet with both hands resting on the table. Thus they stood looking at each other.

"*Plait-il? Je ne comprends pas,*" the Belgian said in bewilderment, and the girl begged:

"Oh, Karl, don't be like that!"

Karl shook his head.

"You're going home," he said. "Mahler, go take my fiancée home."

The other young mechanic got up at once and so did the girl, saying again, "But, Karl—"

She had tears in her eyes. At the surrounding tables people had begun to take notice. Some of them were standing up and craning their heads to see what was going on.

"Come on, come along," said Mahler. He took the girl by the arm and led her toward the exit.

The Belgian was still standing there. Obviously he didn't understand what was going on. The other customers started crowding around our table.

From the Belgian's table another man got up. With a sweeping gesture he pushed the people aside and stepped up to our table.

"What's going on here?" he asked in hard, guttural German.

He was an older man, as tall as the lieutenant, but massive, broad-shouldered and heavy. The lieutenant began to explain. He spoke so fast that I could not follow him.

"Why did you send the lady away?" the second Belgian asked Kruppke.

"Because I don't want my fiancée to dance with a Belgian."

"And why not?"

"Because she is too good for that."

The next thing happened lightning quick. The Belgian raised his arm to strike, but I was a little faster. Jumping up, I struck him in the face from below. I meant to hit him on the chin, but I hit his nose instead. There was a crunching sound, the colossus reeled back and fell crashing to the floor. A few people screamed. . . . I stood there numb. But now Kruppke sprang into action. He kicked the table so that it turned over, grabbed my hand and shouted, "Come on, let's get out of here!"

We ran through the restaurant while people shouted back and forth, and dashed through the glass door into the night, running down the street until our breath gave out.

It was dark; only a few street lamps were lit. Behind us we heard the cries of people pursuing us. We turned into a side street—then we were lost in the labyrinth of the narrow little streets near the cathedral.

Here everything was pitch dark and so silent that we could hear our own heartbeats. We stood for a while and listened, but we could no longer hear our pursuers.

"You've got to get away, Rudi, this very night," Kruppke said. Side by side we went toward the cathedral, calmly, like two peaceful citizens out for an evening walk.

"They'll look for you until they've found you and then. . . ." Kruppke fell silent.

"It was self-defense," I said.

Kruppke shrugged. "Try and explain that to them. The other day they arrested a guy from the Karl Alexander Mine, an old fellow. He had slapped a corporal for being fresh to his daughter. Trial? No. They merely kept him in the guardhouse for one night. And the next morning his own wife didn't recognize him."

It was true. I'd heard similar stories repeated day after day, each grimmer than the last.

"And you?"

"I didn't touch him," Kruppke said. "Everybody saw that."

A Belgian patrol came around the corner. From quite a distance we heard their hobnailed boots resounding on the cobblestones. We pressed ourselves into the shadow of a doorway. There were seven of them, including a sergeant. They didn't see us, but marched past us in the middle of the street, their carbines on their shoulders. Moonlight glinted on the polished steel of the bayonets. Only when their steps had faded into the distance did we come out of the doorway and resume our walk.

"You've got to get out of Aachen," Kruppke urged. "Really, you must get away."

When we turned into my street, we saw light in the attic where I lived. As if on command we both stopped and Kruppke said tightly, "You see, they're already up there."

We turned and ran back down the street. Kruppke lived with his brother atop the garages in a large courtyard at Annunciatenbach. The yard was empty and dark, only a small, red night light glowed over the iron sliding doors leading to the garages. Kruppke disappeared in a woodshed and came back with a motorcycle. It was an NSU and I knew it was his proudest possession.

"You can return it to me once you're out of here."

He shook my hand. I felt a few bills rustle between my fingers —ten thousand paper marks, half his week's wages. My throat tightened. In the light of the night lamp his face looked haggard, hollow.

"But I can't do that," I said.

"Come now, don't talk rot," he said almost angrily.

He escorted me out into the street and we shook hands again in silence. Then I roared off.

At the end of the street I looked around once more. He was still standing there, small, skinny, bent from overwork, waving to me with his large hands. I had worked with him only a year but I felt as if I'd left a brother behind.

When I came out of the city, bright moonlight gleamed on

the road and a cold wind blew from the Eifel Mountains. It was March. The trees were still naked and I froze in the thin, blue Sunday suit in which I'd run out of the Kakadu. Toward seven A.M. I arrived in Remagen. The city was still half asleep. The gaslights shimmered faintly as if about to go out. The streets were empty except for a few workers hurrying off to the morning shift, rushing like shadows along the houses.

I went down the road along the Rhine and stopped in front of our house. I leaned the motorcycle against the stone steps, went up and pushed the bell. The sound of the bell shrilled through the silent hall. After a while I heard soft steps, and a frightened voice asked from behind the door, "Who is there?"

"It's me—Rudi."

The door was unlocked. My sister was standing there in her nightgown, barefooted.

"Rudi! You? For heaven's sake, what is the matter?"

"Had a fight with a Belgian," I said and stepped inside.

She looked at me half shocked, half admiring.

From upstairs came my mother's voice:

"What is it, Hertha?"

I ran up the stairs, three at a time, and then we were in each other's arms. How small she was, how fragile! I saw the many gray strands in her hair. She combed them under when she made up her hair for the day.

She took my face in both hands and held it away from her.

"Done something foolish, my boy?"

"It wasn't as bad as all that. Just a little private argument with Belgians."

I saw the wrinkles deepening around her fine, dark eyes.

"Well, in that case, why don't you go up to your room and freshen up a little? In half an hour we can have breakfast. Then you can tell me all about it."

A little later we sat around the breakfast table and I reported. When I had finished nobody said anything. Finally my brother said pointedly:

"You don't seem aware of the consequences of your actions. It's of course impossible for you to stay here in Remagen. We, too, live in occupied territory and you could bring the worst troubles upon the family."

My brother was then twenty-six years old, six years older than I, and, since my father's death, the senior executive of the firm. He had the unclouded self-esteem of a young man whom fate had put a trifle too soon up on the captain's bridge.

"Yes, Rudi must go," my mother sadly agreed.

And then she and my sister started to discuss my future. Should I learn the wine business or become a baker, or should I be sent to be an apprentice in a hotel? I listened and didn't say a word. I looked down at the Rhine that flowed past beneath the naked poplars. If it were up to me I could spend every day of my life driving a car. But unfortunately that was no occupation. Finally, when the women had worn themselves out talking, they turned to me for an answer.

"Frankly," I said, "I'd like to stay in the automobile business."

"Do you think that's so easy nowadays?" my brother asked. I shrugged.

"I met a manufacturer on the train," said my sister. "He was tremendously interested in automobiles. Wait a minute, what was his name again. . . ." She ran upstairs and came back with her handbag. She dug out a dusty old calling card and we all read it:

> Siegfried Theodor Rathmann
> Manufacturer
> Dresden

"You see, he doesn't even have to give a street, that's how well known he is there," Ilse said proudly.

So it happened that two days later I sat in a train with 60,000 paper marks in my pocket and a promissory note on the future made out to

> S. T. Rathmann, Dresden, Manufacturer.

2

I went directly from the station to Rathmann. The factory was in the old part of the city of Dresden and the sight of it was a great disappointment to me. The entire enterprise consisted of three rooms in the back of a gray tenement.

A young man with bushy blond hair and twinkling blue eyes behind rimless glasses sat in the office.

"Who may I say is calling?" he inquired.

"Caracciola, from Remagen," I said.

He got up and came toward me with his hands held out. "Your sister has already written me."

I looked at him in astonishment.

"Oh," he laughed. "You see, it's me, personally. I'm Rathmann."

With one sweep of his hand he brushed a batch of dolls' torsos off a chair and offered me a seat. I looked around. It was a small, dimly lit room with an old-fashioned desk in the middle, on which ledgers, the remains of a breakfast, and dolls' torsos were heaped helter-skelter. On the floor, too, and on the large shelves along the wall, stood little wooden dolls that stared at me with stupid blue eyes.

"Yes," Rathmann said gaily. "I'm manufacturing wooden dolls now. A week ago it was bowling pins and—who knows? —in another week it may be coffin lids. These days one has to be versatile." He offered me a cigarette. "And now how about you? What have you been doing until now?"

I told him.

"Hm," he said when I'd finished, "and other than that you've no technical skills? I mean, other than automobile mechanics?"

"Oh yes, once I stopped the power plant at Remagen."

"You did? How did that happen?"

I told him the story. In our hotel was the power plant that supplied all Remagen with electricity, including the only movie theater in town. But the movie theater was in the Catholic YMCA and as a Protestant student I couldn't go there. Their priest wouldn't admit me. So several times when they planned to show a movie, I turned off the electricity. A week later I had permanent free passes for myself and all my brothers and sisters, and a month after that I was the movie operator in the Catholic theater.

Rathmann laughed. "That's nice for a start," he said. "But now what?"

I shrugged.

"Well, what sort of plans do you have in mind?"

"I'd like to become a racing-car driver," I said. "If that's impossible I don't care what I do."

"Have you ever been in a race?"

"Of course. Last year I won the prize for midget cars with a 1½-liter Fafnir on the Opel course."

"That's great," said Rathmann. "That's really great. I'll have to introduce you tonight to the members of our group. They're all passionate automobile drivers, although none of them has ever won a prize. But they're all very much interested. I'm sure that one of us can help you."

We made a date for the evening. I was to meet him in front of the Braustube where they regularly met at a reserved table.

Rathmann was half an hour late. On the floor above his "factory" a pipe had burst and the water had drenched his dolls. He had had to dry them first, and even so he was afraid their wooden heads would swell up. He told it like a joke.

We went into the restaurant. In one corner, underneath a green, low-hung lamp, was the roundtable. There were three of them, all young men—Assessor Prickel; Kleeberg, a businessman; and the bank clerk, Scholz. Rathmann was the oldest of them and he introduced me to the others:

"Herr Caracciola, the winner of the Opel course."

"That's wonderful," said Prickel. "I've raced a few times myself. Last year at the Silesian Mountain race. . . ."

"He was eighth in a group of ten announced vehicles," said Kleeberg, "because two competitors withdrew at the last minute."

"And at the previous race Kleeberg withdrew even before the start," said Prickel. "He had made sure to forget his car keys."

Everybody laughed.

"Now let's be serious, gentlemen," Rathmann said, knocking on the table with his signet ring. "We'll have to help Caracciola."

He explained my situation to them. They all grew thoughtful. It was no joke to be without a job in times like these.

"Wouldn't it be best if you approached Fafnir again?" said Scholz. "Perhaps they need a representative here."

Rathmann slapped his forehead. "Of course, that's it—a sales representative for Fafnir. A friend of mine represents another make—three years ago the man started and now he has his own house."

Kleeberg interrupted him. "Wouldn't it be best if Herr Caracciola wrote to his firm soon?"

"Soon?" Rathmann said. "Soon? He is going to write at once."

He called the waiter over and asked for ink, pen and paper.

The waiter brought them on a green blotting pad, setting it down before me on Rathmann's order.

"All right—start then," Rathmann ordered. He took a few hasty drags on his cigarette and began to dictate:

"Dear Mr. Director General:"

"Fafnir has only a director," I interrupted,

"Never mind, leave the Director General, it'll flatter the man and it won't hurt you."

"I'd write 'esteemed,' " said Kleeberg. "That makes it sound more personal."

"With my far-reaching connections among the Dresden business world. . . ." Rathmann went on dictating.

". . . and the heads of local government," Assessor Prickel added, pointing to himself.

They all cooperated and after two hours the letter was ready. I copied it on a clean sheet. After deleting all extraneous suggestions and corrections it boiled down to five sentences. I was merely asking in a brief, dry manner whether the firm would want me to act as their representative and what guarantee would they offer and how much would they pay. Three days later came the answer. The firm was willing to take me on as their representative and to have me sell their cars, but they would not offer a guarantee. "In view of the connections described by you it will be easy for you to earn such high commissions that our guarantee would be superfluous anyhow."

Thus I became a Fafnir representative. I had cards printed and writing paper on which an enormous black letterhead proclaimed:

Rudolf Caracciola

Representative, Fafnir Automobile Works

Dresden   Reitergasse 12.

I should have liked a telephone but that was unfortunately too expensive. I had to be content with sending greetings to my friends and relatives on the Fafnir letterhead. The calling cards I dropped off, on occasional walks, in the mailboxes of rich people. Then I went home to sit in my little room and wait. But no one came.

Times were bad. The roll of paper money I had brought along and kept in a tin box shrank every day. I was nibbling at it on the one hand; on the other hand, inflation ate great chunks away—and inflation had the sharper teeth. I always slept late to save breakfast. I got up at twelve and went straight to lunch. Sometimes the firm inquired whether I had sold anything yet. At first I replied to those inquiries with apologies—later on I simply kept silent.

Only once did I manage to sell a Fafnir to a man. He was a butcher. Kleeberg had happened to overhear in his store that the man wanted to buy a car. I went to him with the catalogue. He looked the cars over, pulled out his wallet and paid the entire price in cash. By the time the car was delivered the money was just enough to pay for the horn and two headlights.

From Aachen the firm managed to reach me long distance. A gruff gentleman asked if I was aware of the inflation, or whether I was too moronic to notice. In the future I could sell only on a dollar basis. And on that basis nobody bought another Fafnir from me.

3

One evening Prickel came to the table, exclaiming: "I've got something for you, Caracciola." He handed me a newspaper. One section was marked red: the German Automobile Club had announced a race for small cars in the Berlin Stadium. I shrugged my shoulders and handed him back the paper.

"They'll hardly let me start on foot. . . ."

"But surely, Fafnir will—"

"Out of the question," I said. "Not after that fiasco the other day."

Kleeberg spoke up.

"I think I can get you a car."

"And how much would that cost?"

"Nothing," he said. "Wuesthoff is an old war buddy of mine. One word and he'll lend you his little Ego, I'm sure."

Already the following Sunday I was out in Chemnitz, visiting Wuesthoff. He looked like a young feudal baron, but he had the big heart and the open hand of an old soldier.

"Of course you can have my little Ego," he said.

He went to the garage right away. On the way he gave me some tips. I should drive past the factory in Berlin and have the car overhauled before the race.

"As it is now you can at best compete with a funeral procession," he said.

We shook hands and I drove back to Dresden. In the evening the roundtable received me with much clamor. They bet a small barrel of beer on my victory and supplied me generously with good advice. Rathmann handed me a one-eyed wooden doll for a mascot, and Kleeberg warned me not to sleep with my window open. He was afraid I might catch a cold before the big day. Of course, they all wanted to come to Berlin and watch the race.

"Just to console you afterward," said Prickel, smiling amiably.

The race took place at the end of April. I had left a week before to be there on time. The airplane factory, Merkur, which manufactured the little Ego, was on the east side of Berlin. I was prepared for a fight, but it turned out differently. The sales manager of Ego automobiles, a snappy gentleman with the tips of his mustache pointing upward, had already been informed by Wuesthoff. He received me with roaring good humor.

"So you are our champion for the Sunday race? You've got courage, I must say that, but how about the money?"

I opened my mouth to reply but he made a gesture of dismissal.

"Never mind, it can happen to all of us. We'll do it cheaply for you. My idea is this: if you win with Ego, you needn't pay anything; if you lose you'll have to pay for the spare parts needed for the overhaul."

I thanked him and we shook hands on the deal.

The following days I spent in the factory from morning till night. Together with the co-driver whom the firm had put at my disposal, I fussed around with the car. The co-driver was a cheerful Berlin boy.

"You know," he said, "not that you can brag about an old piece of junk like that, but when you see the other cars in the contest, you can sleep in peace. Man, I'm telling you—iron bathtubs on four wheels!"

Since a large number of small cars had registered, three qualifying runs had to be driven Saturday afternoon. The winners were to start for the final contest on Sunday. The stadium looked like an enormous dried-up swimming pool, the cement glistening white in the sun. The stands were almost empty. Only up in the boxes little groups of people sat here and there. In the vast expanse they looked lost, like forgotten umbrellas.

The drivers were mostly young men out to win their spurs. Many of them were fantastically dressed, with crash helmets and enormous goggles which they didn't take off even while they were having coffee in the restaurant.

They discussed tactical questions with extraordinary vocal volume. Up in the north corner the Patzenhofer Brewery had painted a huge advertisement in large white letters. Now they were arguing whether one should swing down into the straightaway at the P or the A of Patzenhofer. Only one man kept aloof—a gentleman with a button nose, a high stiff collar and cat's whiskers.

"That's engineer Niedlich, drives a special make of Grade," my co-driver whispered. And I watched, full of awed respect, as the great man walked majestically back and forth, his arms crossed. The car alongside him had the form of a flat boat. In the back an enormous exhaust pipe stuck out threateningly, like a torpedo gun.

They divided the drivers of the four-horse-power class by lot. Niedlich got into the first run and I was glad that the dangerous competitor did not start in my group.

The first ones rolled to the start. The motors thundered and the hot smell of fuel blew into my nostrils. Niedlich's Grade roared loud enough for three. He filled the huge cement pool of the stadium with its ear-splitting drone and the enormous exhaust pipe spewed clouds of ill-smelling fumes.

They raced off, Niedlich ahead of the others. They moved along the straightaway, went into the turn at the opposite end, crawling like flies over the Patzenhofer sign and then they returned, rattling and coughing. Next to me stood a reporter. Over his shoulder I saw him write:

"A breath-taking sight, the cars chasing around the steep curves at 75 kilometers per hour. . . ."

Niedlich won the first practice run.

Then my group went to the start. I competed against two Cocos and one Omikron. When I settled down behind the wheel I had a strange feeling in my stomach, the same feeling I used to have at the end of the school year, at Easter, when I was called into the principal's office after the teachers' conference.

A gentleman in a cutaway lowered the flag and we were off. Forty laps had to be covered; forty laps—26.6 kilometers. The course was divided by three white lines. Most of the drivers shot up into the incline at the turns and then like hawks swooped down into the straightaway. It looked very dramatic but it cost a lot of time. I therefore decided to stay in the middle field because, below, the turns didn't permit greater speeds. I stepped on the gas as hard as my calf muscles permitted and the speedometer trembled up to 77 kilometers. After the sixth lap the co-driver shouted, "Slow down! We've passed all of them."

I dropped down to 70 and so we drove the race home. When we arrived at the finish line a few people congratulated me first and I had to spell my name for a reporter. We climbed out of the car and the co-driver checked the motor. The oil had heated up; it was spraying and hissing from the valves.

"Well, then you'll have to blow air into the crank case, Schulz," I told the co-driver. He nodded resignedly.

And then came the day of the race.

On the way to the stadium we saw that it was going to be a real public festival. All Berlin seemed to be on its feet with wives and children and sandwich packages. The arena now re-

sembled an enormous crater overrun by black and white insects
and above it a burning sun stood in the thunder-clouded sky.

First, the motorcycles ran. Under ordinary circumstances the
outcome of that race would have interested me enormously. But
at the moment I wished only that it were over and that we
ourselves could start.

Finally the word came down: Get ready to go.

There were four of us. Niedlich in a Grade, Huettner in an
Omikron, Hoffman in a Coco and I in Wuesthoff's little Ego.
The drivers were as unknown as the car makes. At the start
there were a few reporters; also the gentleman in the cutaway
was back again. He looked like a June bug walking on its hind
legs. He loaded us with advice, such as that one must let a competitor pass if he wants to, and that one must protest irregular-
ities not during but after the race. We hardly listened, and
climbed into our cars. Next to me was Niedlich. He sat motionless at the wheel, staring straight ahead.

The engines began to roar and once again Niedlich's Grade
outroared all of us. Then we were off.

I had only one thought: to take the lead, keep in front and
drive always in the center lane.

In the rear-view mirror I saw Niedlich roaring along, surrounded by a cloud of steam, a fire-spitting volcano on wheels.
Alongside me Schulz, sweating and panting, was pumping air
into the crank case.

Then the Grade car disappeared from the mirror and Hoffmann's Coco moved into the picture. I stepped on the gas and
the Coco vanished too.

I was keyed up with excitement. The motor droned in my
ears like a second, louder heart in addition to my own.

"I can't keep it up," Schulz panted. "My arm!"

"You've got to!" I shouted. Then Niedlich reappeared. He
was now hovering like a hawk above me in the steep turn. I
stepped on the gas as hard as I could and Schulz pumped like

a doomed sailor in a leaking vessel. When we passed the turn the next time, I had reached the P of Patzenhofer while Niedlich was still rushing across the A. Thus I fought forward, letter by letter.

"Which lap is this?"

"The thirty-eighth."

"No, only the thirty-seventh," I told him. But Schulz shook his head, his teeth clenched.

Then, two laps later, the gentleman in the cutaway stepped out into the course. He was holding a flag in front of him—the finish! Thank God, the finish. . . .

We roared past him into the infield. I braked; the car stopped.

"You see, I said it was thirty-eight!" said Schulz.

At the next instant we were drowned in a mass of people. They crowded around the car, they laughed, shook our hands, slapped our shoulders and shouted so loudly that it was impossible to understand what anyone was saying. The cat-whiskered director of Ego parted the crowd like a swimmer. He approached me, lifted me from the car, embraced me and pressed his mustache against my cheek.

"Fabulous, my boy," he said. "Just fabulous. If we ever start a racing department you can become driver for us."

At that moment Niedlich's Grade thundered up. He stopped right next to me. I saw him pushing himself up on the back of the seat and I heard him explain loudly to those about him:

"If my mechanic hadn't forgotten to release the hand brake, Mr. Caracciola wouldn't be standing here as the victor. Unfortunately I noticed the oversight only after three quarters of the first lap."

He got out of his car and disappeared in the crowd.

Then suddenly the fellows from the roundtable were there. They had come down from the stands. Kleeberg and Schulz were carrying an enormous laurel wreath. They hung it over the front of the car and Rathmann stepped forward, handed me a free subscription to twelve noontime meals and said:

"Rudolf Caracciola, at first you were an alien branch on our tree. But from today on you are counted as one of us. You could qualify as a Saxon, no, even a Dresden man. . . ."

He didn't get to finish his speech. The course was declared free and we drove the honor lap. Very slowly we drove around the great oval that now lay so gay and friendly in the sun. How the people enjoyed themselves! They jumped from their seats, waved and shouted, and a bouquet of flowers hit me on the side of the head. I was grateful and touched and even Schulz said it was the second most beautiful moment of his life.

After the honor lap we drove out of the stadium through the tunnel. In the tunnel it was cool and still. A shadow detached itself from the darkness, stepped in our path.

"One moment, please," he said.

We stopped.

A tall gentleman, dressed formally in black, came to the car, put a hand on the steering wheel, bowed and said:

"I'm from the race management. There has been formal objection to your victory."

"Why—how. . . ." I was completely perplexed.

"I said," he repeated in a sharper tone, "that there has been a protest against your victory."

"Who protested it?"

"I am not in the position to tell you that. At any rate, there is a suspicion that you have not registered the cylinder size of your car correctly. Will you please follow me?"

He went ahead, and we drove slowly behind him. Schulz was cursing softly. Right outside the tunnel our guide turned to the left and led us into the twilight of a pit. Two other gentlemen were waiting there. We had to get out of the car, open the hood and unscrew the cylinder head.

Then one of the three came up slowly, with precise gait, and lowered the measuring rod into the cylinder. He pulled it out, held it against the light and gave a sign of regret to someone standing behind me. I turned around and caught a last glimpse of the mustached cat's head of Mr. Niedlich disappearing.

The man turned to us.

"We apologize," he said. "Unfortunately we've been wrongly informed. The cylinder capacity as registered by you is correct."

All three bowed like puppets on a string and disappeared through a door in the background of the pit.

"Niedlich drives a Grade straight and goes crooked," punned Schulz while we screwed the top back on the cylinder. I was a little depressed. It was a blight on the first joy of victory. But then, when we emerged from the twilit pit back into the sun where friends were waiting with the hard-earned little barrel of beer, everything was quickly forgotten.

Because I was young and I had won.

4

I sat staring at the brown, leather-upholstered door behind which Herzing had disappeared. He had been gone for at least half an hour and I felt that I could not bear this sitting and waiting any longer. The blond secretary behind the railing pretended to be very busy. She wrote something, made entries in a book, went to get a rubber stamp and sat down behind her typewriter again. She was very pretty and rather haughty. She hardly seemed to notice me.

Outside it was raining. I saw the raindrops spattering against the window, and just in front of the window a poplar bent with the rain and each leaf trembled under the falling drops.

From where I sat I could see part of the factory yard— three long, low hangars with glass roofs above them. They looked like hothouse beds from this distance.

Everything had happened very suddenly. Actually, even surprising to myself. One day Wuesthoff had introduced me to Director Herzing of the Daimler works and I had told him that I wanted more than anything to become a racing driver and to drive for Daimler.

So here I sat now in the plant at Untertuerkheim and waited.

The upholstered door looked heavy and stately, as in a doctor's waiting room. And behind that door sat Director Herzing and Director Gross discussing my fate.

"Would you mind asking, Miss . . ."

"Schroeder," the blond lady said and looked at me severely. "No! Director Gross has given orders never to be disturbed during a meeting."

She talked across her typewriter while she was putting in a new sheet. Then she started hammering away. She did not seem inclined to converse with me any further.

On the wall across from me hung a picture and a large calendar. The picture portrayed a gentleman with a long beard, probably the founder of the firm. The calendar told me it was June 11. My mother's birthday was a few days off. It would be nice if I could go to her and say, "Look here, Mama, now I'm a racing driver with Mercedes. A thousand marks a month to begin with—starting premiums and prizes extra, of course." She would be so touched she would weep; I'm sure she would weep knowing that something had become of me after all.

A pity that I could not represent my own case behind that upholstered door. Surely Herzing was much too wishy-washy once he met any resistance. I should go about it in an entirely different manner.

"*Herr Direktor*," I would say, "just trust me with one of your cars once—only once for a test, and you can be sure I'll return the winner or else I shan't ever drive in a race again."

The telephone rang. The blond secretary took the receiver off the cradle, listened, said "Yes" and again, "Yes, *Herr Direktor!*" and put the receiver down again.

"You're to go downstairs to Mr. Werner. He's at the main entrance.

She pushed a bell and an office boy appeared.

"Take the gentleman down to the factory, Werner," she said and went back to her work. I walked behind the box. My heart was pounding in my throat. So now my fate would be decided. Within the next half hour I would know whether

I could really drive, whether I had the stuff to win a Grand Prix or whether all these were daydreams, silly hallucinations with which I'd fooled myself.

Werner was going to test me—the great Werner, winner of so many racing contests. He was one of the hard men of the old guard who had thundered along the country roads in their high-wheeled, springless vehicles. Often they had reached the finish line with hands like raw lumps of meat, battered by the knocks of the steering wheel, but even so they'd made 150 kilometers and more.

We crossed the yard. It was still raining. Clashing noises came from the hangars and sometimes the ground under our feet throbbed with the poundings of a great machine.

In front of a shed stood the chassis of a car minus the body. Only the chassis frame with makeshift wooden seats. We stopped. From the dim light of the shed a tall, gaunt man emerged, dressed in blue overalls. It was Werner.

"Good day," he said and shook my hand. Silently he pointed to the driver's seat on the chassis and silently he sat down next to me. He had a long, sad face with a large nose and deep-set eyes. It was a face that looked as if it would never laugh again.

We took off. Werner gave the orders.

"Turn right, straight ahead, swing over to the left. . . ."

I showed him what I could do. I drove down the straight roads as if they were a race track and I went around the corners so that the rainwater under the rear wheels spurted high. After half an hour Werner gave the sign to turn back and we drove back to the plant. At the main entrance he got out. He shook my hand.

"*Gruess Gott!*" he said and turned to go.

"And how was it?" I called after him.

"I'll tell them upstairs," he said and vanished in the darkness of the shed.

I stayed nervously behind. Was he so disappointed in me

that he wouldn't even say one word to me? I went to the guard at the entrance and called the office from there. They were still in conference.

"You can wait down there meanwhile," said the secretary. "*Herr Direktor* Gross has been informed."

I was rather depressed. Obviously Werner's opinion had been bad enough for them to treat me so offhandedly now.

It was now half-past five. The stream of employees had dribbled away to nothing. The guard sat in his little cubicle and stealthily dunked a fresh roll into a cup of coffee. I sat down with him and we started to chat. We talked about Werner.

"A great fellow, that," he said. "Unfortunately he's terribly unhappy. His wife died not very long ago."

At last the phone rang. He reached for the receiver and then told me, "You're to come upstairs right away. But hurry, they're about to leave."

I ran up to the office. I was still a little excited but not as much as before. The long waiting had numbed me and, all in all, I had little hope left.

The upholstered door to the inner sanctum was now open and inside the two gentlemen stood talking. They were indeed ready to leave. Herzing had his coat over his arm and was talking to a man in a raincoat who stood beside him— a big-shouldered, massive figure. That was Director Gross.

"There's that boy!" he roared when he saw me. "Well then, Werner was quite satisfied with you. You can start in Dresden. As a salesman. A hundred marks a month."

I was about to say something, but Herzing threw me a warning look. As we walked downstairs I whispered to him, behind the giant's back:

"But I wanted to be a racing driver—"

"Don't be an idiot," Herzing replied, also in a whisper. "Racing is no profession. First be an employee of the firm, then one day perhaps you can drive as much as you want."

5

I had been in the salesroom for three months and still hadn't sold anything. It was a fabulous place, just opposite the European Hotel. Our clientele was the most select.

Sundays I was occasionally permitted to borrow a sports car and to participate in a race. Those weren't big events—just minor local races. I won most of the time, but that didn't change my situation. I was—and remained—the salesman Rudolf Caracciola with a hundred marks salary and a claim to one and a half per cent commission for every car sold through my initiative.

Unfortunately, no commission was ever pocketed by me. Each time I softened up a customer with my sales talk, Herzing appeared from the office and closed the deal himself. Afterward he patted me on the shoulder and told me to keep up the good work.

There were three of us salesmen in the showroom. The other two were older and more experienced than I. When we had nothing to do we would stand around in our excellent blue flannel jackets cracking jokes and making remarks about the people strolling outside the window.

My two colleagues seemed very worldly wise. They could appraise the worth of a woman on sight and were uncannily expert in guessing her qualities and weaknesses. During such conversations I kept quiet because I didn't want to make a fool of myself. I'd have liked a girl, too, and I'd even seen one I liked very much. She lived at the European Hotel. Sometimes I saw her by her window on the second floor, wearing a light dress, staring down into the street. At first I watched her from the back of the showroom, then I went up to the display window and smiled up at her. She smiled back, then vanished behind the curtain.

Occasionally I saw her leaving the hotel accompanied by an older gentleman. They'd go over to their car, and the porter would open the door for them and bow. I inquired about them and learned that he was a Berlin businessman and she was a friend. Her name was Charly. The name Charly pleased me enormously.

For a few days I didn't see her at all. When we met again, I smiled at her openly and bowed a little; she smiled back and gave a little nod. Otherwise nothing happened. She'd stand there at the window of the hotel, and I down in the showroom. Eventually I opened my heart to our senior salesman, Heinz von Berck. He was twenty-eight years old and a member of an old, respected family. He suggested that I go to the tea dance which was held every afternoon at the European Hotel. He would go along and pretend to be interested in Charly, while I remained in the background.

"That's the way to do if you want to get a woman crazy about you," he told me—and he knew all about it.

On Wednesday afternoon we went to the hotel. It was a rainy day. The great hall where the tea dance was held looked rather gloomy. She was there.

We sat down not far from her and von Berck waggled his wrist, on which he wore a gold chain bracelet, and ordered tea. Then the music began—a slow fox trot—and Berck approached and asked Charly for a dance, just as we had planned. My eyes followed them as they went gliding over the parquet. She had a very pretty, graceful figure. She and Heinz made an attractive couple on the dance floor.

The music stopped. He came back to the table, mopped his forehead with a perfumed handkerchief and said, "The next dance is yours. Make the most of it, Caracciola."

The dance was a tango. I went over to her feeling a little shaky in the knees. She nodded, arose with a smile, and soon we were dancing together.

"Do you drive a car, too?" I asked.

"No," she said.

"But you're interested in the automobile sport?"

"A little," she said.

The saxophone player put down his instrument and held a megaphone to his mouth. " 'Because I love you. . . .' " he sang meltingly and, once again, like a sigh: " 'I love you. . . .' " It was exactly what I wanted to say.

She smiled. "But you are a great racing driver, aren't you?"

"Well, so-so," I said.

"Your friend told me about you."

"He did?"

" 'I can't forget. . . .' " the saxophone player sang into his megaphone. From her dress and from her hair rose a fine, vagrant scent of verbena, almost imperceptible.

"You're not very talkative," she remarked.

I smiled awkwardly. "I'd like you to watch me racing some day," I said.

"Why?"

"Because then I think you'd have more regard for me." It sounded very clumsy and my voice was completely hoarse.

For a moment she looked at me astonished, then she laughed. She had pretty, even teeth and when she laughed I could see the rosy inside of her mouth. The dance was over and I escorted her back to her table.

"Well, how did it go?" asked von Berck.

I shrugged and said nothing. It was impossible for me to say anything just then.

We left soon after. And in the days that followed Charly and I met again and again, until she left Dresden.

It was some weeks later that I won the flat race in Freiburg and another race at Forstenried. There were laurel wreaths and beautiful silver cups, but you can't support a woman on those.

I'd have liked to enter my name for one of the Grand Prix but there was no question of that. When I mentioned it to Herzing, he immediately shook his head. With the big racing cars one could not experiment, he said; they had to be left in the hands of the old guard.

What I had not dared to hope almost happened anyhow. My successes during the year of 1924 did not go unnoticed. I was first in the Prague mountain race—the best in my class and the best time of the day.

Then I drove the race in Nideggen, in the Eifel—another mountainous course. The difficult, tortuous course could be compared with the Targa-Florio in Sicily. Except for two short straight runs there were eighty curves in each lap.

The race for touring and sports cars took place on a Saturday. The weather had been cold and windy during the training. On the day of the race it was even worse, approaching a storm. The wind whipped across the road in gusts. A sudden squall caught me sideways and I was pulled off course and thrown against a tree. The car was a mess, and I had intended to start with this car the next morning in the racing-car category.

However, I was lucky once again. After the race the car was hauled off to Cologne and repaired there overnight. Headlights and mudguards had to be removed. Sunday morning, there I was in my Mercedes, fit and ready to go. I won the race and with it the 1924 German Tourist Trophy.

In the evening I went home to Remagen where my mother received me with a big hug.

In August the Klausen Pass race in Switzerland took place. The course is almost twenty-two kilometers long—the longest and, I would say, the most beautiful and most diversified of all mountain courses. The Mercedes team was fully represented. Salzer and Merz drove racing cars, I, sports cars; many private drivers, including a gentleman-farmer named Kluge, a paper manufacturer, Clemm, and Adolf Rosenberger drove Mercedes sports cars. It was a Mercedes invasion. Director Max Sailer was our sponsor. He arrived with a big, six-cylinder chassis, built by Dr. Porsche. On top of the chassis an enormous crate was mounted, which contained every imaginable spare part for our cars.

We all met in a little hotel in the Lin Valley, at the foot of Klausen Pass. After the hours of training we gathered in the taproom, a cozy place if somewhat noisy, paneled in pale wood and with tables to match.

Otto Merz was usually the chief figure among the noisy, laughing drivers. He was as strong as a bear and he loved to show off his strength. While I was sitting at the table, minding my own business, his big hand reached through my legs to the back rung of the chair and thus lifted me bodily, holding me up in the air, with me kicking and laughing. Kluge, Clemm, Rosenberger and many others surrounded Merz and gaped at him until he put me down.

"Gentlemen," he cried, "who wants to take me up on a bet? I'll take this nail and slam it through the top of the table so that the tip of the nail emerges beneath. For each millimeter the nail is driven through the wood, I get a bottle of champagne."

Murmurs of disbelief. The table was about two inches thick. I kept my mouth shut. I knew Merz could do it; I'd seen it.

"Okay, I'll take you on," said Kluge. "Even if it costs me ten bottles of champagne, I'd like to see you do it!"

Merz took a thick, five- to six-inch nail, held it between his third and ring finger, pressed the head of the nail into the heel of his hand and raised his arm to strike. The impact thundered through the room. The nail was in. Pretty far in, in fact. We turned the table around and found the tip of the nail protruding—about four millimeters. Kluge ordered four bottles of champagne, which we decided to drink the following day either to celebrate victory or to console ourselves in defeat. It turned out that the bottles were drunk to victory because Merz was first in the racing-car class and I was winner in the sports-car class.

Finally the big day came which was to bring fulfillment of my fondest hopes: participation in the 800-kilometer Grand Prix of Italy. I was to be the alternate driver to start with, but nevertheless a participant.

The main drivers were Werner, the winner in the Targa-Florio race, Alfred Neubauer, and the amateur drivers Count Masetti of Italy and Count Zborowski of England. These were to drive the new 8-cylinder 2-liter Mercedes cars which Dr. Porsche had built. Two weeks before the race we were on our way to Monza. I was assigned the big 6-cylinder chassis with the spare-parts crate that I was to take safely and intact to Monza. Neubauer was to meet me in Switzerland on the first night en route.

"Werner always goes into one of those little inns in the Sihl Valley, in Sihlbrugg," he said. "Let's go there too because I'm sure they must have an excellent cook. The next day we'll go across the Gotthard Pass to Milan."

So we decided to stay overnight in Sihlbrugg.

As soon as we sat down at the table, Neubauer called the waitress over.

"Listen, miss, what kind of wine does Mr. Werner usually drink when he stays here?"

"Mr. Werner?" she giggled. "He never drinks anything but champagne."

The drive across the Gotthard with the chassis and the heavy crate was no joy ride. The car was anything but curve-happy, and I had to work with both arms to steer the stubborn thing up and down over the rocky, narrow, dust-covered pass. We arrived in the evening, tired, dirty, but in one piece. The Hotel Marchesi, where we had reservations, was idyllically situated on the edge of Monza's park. Since singles were not available, Neubauer and I shared a room.

The mosquitoes in the park were very bad. In spite of the heavy curtains, hordes of the bloodthirsty creatures got in and clung to the white walls.

When it was time to go to bed, Neubauer and I sneaked into the room without turning on the lights. I rushed to the window and shut it. Neubauer, who waited at the door, turned the light on. And then we began, each with a slipper in hand, and swatted them on every wall. By standing on the bed we could even reach those on the ceiling. We must have slain at least sixty mosquitoes. The walls showed that previous guests had waged similar battles. At any rate, we were able to sleep in peace.

During practice I didn't get to drive at all. There were so many things wrong with the cars that even the first string drivers hardly had time for practice. I sat around looking at the Alfa Romeos which, compared to our cars, looked much more capable.

Ascari was an impressive-looking man. He drove the Alfa and he was the most feared competitor.

On October 19, 1924, at ten in the morning, the 800-kilometer race for the Grand Prix of Italy began. Ascari took off like a fire engine. I had the best spectator's seat, atop the roof above our pit. Werner and Count Zborowski didn't get off right away; their motors refused to start. But finally they did and Werner was off, followed soon after by Zborowski.

Ascari of Alfa Romeo was clear in the lead. Behind him came Campari and Wagner, then Masetti, all of Mercedes.

In the next group came Minoia, Neubauer and Werner. During the seventeenth lap Werner pulled up at the pit. Change of spark plugs. A loss of five to eight minutes.

"Caracciola," Sailer called. "Come on, come on down! Take over!"

I pretended the noise of the motors had drowned out his words and by the time I slowly lowered myself off the roof, Werner was already gone. I was in no mood to carry on the hopeless battle.

Neubauer stopped. Change of spark plugs. Merz stopped. Spark plugs. Werner, too, pulled up again.

Ascari flew along the course and drove the record lap of the day—167 kilometers.

After 400 kilometers the Alfa Romeos pulled up at the boxes for refueling. Ascari, afterward, was in too much of a hurry to start. He forgot the weight of the full tank. In the turn following the straightaway it nearly got him—the car skidded, bolted, but Ascari caught it just in time before it got entirely out of control. Count Masetti dropped out in the 42nd lap. His gas line was broken. Zborowski refueled in the 47th lap and changed tires. Then he raced off after Ascari. No sooner had he disappeared behind the first curve than we saw a cloud of dust. People started running and waving their arms. Zborowski had crashed badly. In the famous, much-feared narrow Lesmo turn his right front tire blew and the car crashed into a pole. He was taken to the hospital with a fractured skull and died soon after.

Ascari drove across the finish line a few laps ahead of everyone else. It was then we got word of Zborowski's death. Max Sailer raised the flag to stop Werner and Neubauer as a token of mourning for a dead teammate and a great sportsman.

At the beginning of the century Count Zborowski's father had suffered a fatal accident in the south of France. He had been driving a Mercedes in a mountain race. The cause of the accident was supposed to have been a cuff link that got caught in the steering wheel and thus blocked the mechanism for an instant.

Now my first Grand Prix was over and I was actually glad to have been spared the ordeal of driving under those unfortunate circumstances.

The year 1925 brought me eight victories with my Mercedes, among them four mountain races and the over-all victory in the Batschari race at Baden-Baden. But again, this year had not brought me the satisfaction of starting in one of the Grand Prix.

6

In June I heard that the firm did not intend to start their cars in the German Grand Prix on the Avus-Berlin in 1926 because there was another race taking place simultaneously in Spain, and the Spanish race was more important for export considerations.

I asked Herzing for a few days' leave and went to Stuttgart. Just as two years ago, I sat once more before the leather-upholstered door of the director's office. But this time I was shown in and could present my case in person. For two hours I bombarded the director with requests, promises and arguments until finally I banished all his doubts.

At last, I was given a car. However, I was not to start in the name of the firm. I was Rudolf Carraciola—a private entry, starting on his own; and if things went wrong I was—at least to outsiders—to bear the brunt of my defeat. Rosenberger, the other Mercedes driver, drove under the same conditions.

A week before the race I went to Berlin. To save money, I stayed at a small hotel in the center of town. Every morning I drove out to the Avus to practice.

It was a rainy summer, one day as gray as the other and the sun never in view. There was hardly a lap where gusts of rain did not whip across the course. In the evenings I returned to the hotel, drenched and dead tired. I was deeply depressed. According to the gossip around the boxes, Minoia, Chassagne and

Urban-Emmerich had been making much better time than I, and I knew that Rosenberger was faster.

Friday, during training, a dreadful accident occurred. In the south turn Plate and Heine collided. Plate was severely hurt and Pinoli, his co-driver, was killed on the spot. I drove past a minute later. Ambulance men were carrying Plate away while Pinoli lay on the ground where he had fallen.

I got out and looked at him. He was the first dead person I'd ever seen in my life. He was sprawled out on his back, arms flung wide as if he were nailed to an invisible cross. His wide-open eyes reflected the sky. The rain fell in long skeins and ran over his face. Presently an ambulance man came with a piece of canvas and covered him. Only the feet in the white canvas shoes protruded from the covering.

It was a desolate sight. Shuddering, I drove back to the hotel and tried not to think of the white canvas shoes.

Charly arrived that evening. She was cheerful and tense with excitement. She had read all the newspaper accounts about the training, and had marked the places where my name was mentioned. There were not many. The favorites of the press were Rosenberger, Minoia, Ricken on NAG, and Urban-Emmerich. About me they said only that young Caracciola might perhaps create a surprise.

"If you win," said Charly, "you'll get seventeen thousand marks and a gold cup."

She'd learned that from the newspapers.

Sunday started out bright and sunny. The race was to begin at two in the afternoon, but when we drove out to the Avus shortly after one, we saw a leaden wall looming on the western horizon.

The race was run in three classes. First the big cars, then ours. We were posted directly in front of the stands. I tried to spot Charly among the crowd of people, but it was impossible to recognize a single person in the swaying mass of heads.

I looked down the course. The asphalt lay black and smooth in the dim afternoon light. Way off, in the great curve, the big cars were just disappearing. The others started off, but I remained standing on the spot, just in front of the stands. Salzer, my co-driver, turned pale.

The motor had stalled.

"Come on, get out—push!" I shouted at him.

He jumped out, hurried back and started to push the car. I stepped hard on the gas pedal, but the motor didn't respond. I felt my hands turn moist with excitement. Finally the engine caught. With one jump Salzer was beside me. We were off.

We followed the field that had disappeared behind the gray-green wall of pines. I shifted, slowed down, stepped on the gas again—all very mechanically. I was dreadfully depressed. Nothing mattered any more. One of those ahead of me was driving home to victory and all I had to do was to see the battle through with composure. They were at least a minute ahead of me and I knew what Rosenberger could do—and Minoia.

I drove and drove, past the pits, down the straightaway into the south turn, back over the counter straightaway and up near Halensee through the big northern loop.

When I passed the stands for the fourth time it started to rain. First a few large drops that multiplied faster and faster, and then the car swooshed through a veritable flood. In a moment we were wet to the skin. But worst of all—the road had become slippery, as if soaped—that awful slipperiness we had feared even during practice. I drove—and kept driving. . . .

The rain steamed up the windshield and the tires threw up geysers of water. When I came round the next time there was a crowd at the pit and two cars were parked on the green center area. Obviously quite a few had dropped out.

I slowed down somewhat and continued at 160 kilometers. Better to arrive last than to drop out, I thought; I owed that much to the firm.

The eighth round. There, the press gallery . . . the time-keeper's booth. . . .

It hit me like a blow.

A car had smashed into the booth. Glass splinters were strewn around . . . twisted metal. A man lay on the ground and from the stands others came running. I wanted to stop but I had to go on.

"Who was it?" I shouted to Salzer.

"Rosenberger, I think," he shouted back.

Rosenberger. My teammate. So I was the only one still racing for Mercedes.

At the next round I drove up to the pit for gas and oil. Dr. Porsche, our top designer, was there, and Sailer. They were not there officially, however, because I was not racing for Mercedes, but they insisted on taking care of the two protégés of the firm.

I came to a stop.

"What happened?" I asked hastily. "Rosenberger?"

Dr. Porsche nodded.

"Bad?"

"No, just slightly hurt."

I was suspicious, however. The car must have smashed with terrible impact against the little shed.

I was driving again. Across from the press gallery the people were herded in a thick, black cluster. There was an ambulance, and as I raced by I saw them loading somebody on a stretcher.

I drove on.

The rain came streaming down without letup and the course was now so slippery that I could only concentrate on that little black strip of shining asphalt ahead. It glistened like sealskin.

The ninth lap. The tenth. . . . We were chasing down the straightaway. There, on the counter-straightaway, a blue car . . . it started to skid, raced across the green to our side and, like a blue streak, plowed into the spectators.

Don't look back, keep on driving!

"Who was it?"

Salzer shrugged his shoulders.

Eleventh lap. . . .

The engine was no longer working properly—a spark plug failed; we had to drive up to the pits again. The rules said only the driver himself is allowed to make repairs.

I tore open the hood, unscrewed the first spark plug. It was burning hot. I threw it to Dr. Porsche who was standing in the back of the pit. He examined it with a magnifying glass, shook his head and threw it back. The next; the third. My hands began to flutter with nervousness.

"No defect. Can't find anything wrong!" Porsche said.

Outside, the others were racing past, one after the other, motors roaring, pulling a veil of exhaust fumes after them. The fifth spark plug, the sixth, the seventh . . . there, at last, the eighth! I quickly screwed in a new one, threw down the hood and ran back to my seat. Off we went.

"One and a half minutes," said Salzer, and thrust the stop watch back into his windbreaker.

One and a half minutes—wasn't it pointless to drive on at all? Twelfth lap, thirteenth lap. The rain had stopped, but down at the south curve there must have been another accident. The railing behind which the spectators stood was broken and there was a wide gap in the wall of onlookers.

By and by dull, dry spots were appearing in the rainy, glistening skin of the asphalt road. I poured gas into the engine and began to speed up to about 200 kilometers. We were passing other cars, quite a few of them in fact. They were all driving more carefully now; there had been too many accidents. But even at this speed I hadn't a chance to win.

One and a half minutes—I couldn't make up for that!

We were driving, driving, driving . . . I didn't know which place was ours in the field, nor who was behind and ahead of us.

It was a race in the fog, lonely and without orientation, the only compass being one's sense of duty. A few times Sailer waved at me from the boxes. "Faster, hurry up, faster. . . ." But I was already getting all I could out of the engine and I didn't dare force any more speed on the treacherous road.

Eighteenth lap, nineteenth, twentieth—the last. . . . Legs and arms grew heavy, the eyes tired. It was really futile to go on.

There—the finish line.

Brakes—and stop.

Slowly I got up, heavily with trembling legs. I felt dreadful, discouraged, fagged. The wet clothes clung to my body. Suddenly people came running toward me from the pits, the people in the stands got to their feet, gesticulating wildly. Sailer approached at a run.

"Rudi—victory!" He shouted from far away.

The national hymn—the German flag rose on the mast and they put an enormous wreath around my shoulders. I looked at Salzer; Salzer looked at me, and suddenly we both burst out laughing wildly. The people looked at us bewildered, then they started laughing too. Handshakes, flowers, the photographers dancing all around us. We were driving the honor lap.

My eyes searched for Charly. She was not there; she didn't come down from the stands to congratulate me.

I was disappointed. Quickly I said good-by to Dr. Porsche and headed back to the hotel. I wanted to take a bath and put on fresh, dry clothes. I was just in the process of taking off my wet things when there was a knock at the door. Rathmann.

"Rudi," he shouted. "My boy, that was absolutely great! I'm really proud of you."

He came toward me with his arms spread wide. I waved him off.

"Forget it," I said. "I've just been lucky."

He looked around for a chair and then sat down on the bed.

"Well, then, my dear Rudi," he said, "now I'm going to take over the management of your success. You've just earned seventeen thousand marks. I'm going to sell my doll factory tomorrow—that's another seventeen thousand; and we'll throw the money together and open a showroom on the Kurfuersten-damm—Rudolf Caracciola, winner of the Grand Prix of Germany, personally selling automobiles. If that won't draw customers I don't know what will, if I know my Berlin. Okay?"

"I'll think it over," I said hesitantly and with a rather glum shake of my head. At that moment the telephone rang. It was Charly.

"Congratulations," she said. Her voice was without joy.

"What's the matter with you?"

"Oh, nothing."

"Why didn't you come down to me out there?"

"I left earlier," she said.

"Can we meet right away?"

"Yes," she said. "That's why I'm calling."

Half an hour later we met in a restaurant on Potsdamer Platz. The moment she came toward me I saw that she had been crying.

"Charly, what is the matter?"

"Nothing," she said.

"Why did you leave earlier?"

She was trembling from head to toe.

"You know," she said, "I was standing next to Chassagne's wife. You know, the Frenchman who crashed on the eleventh lap. And she was standing there, staring out at the empty course and waiting, waiting, waiting all the time. . . . I could tell that she was praying inside . . . and then they announced it—Chassagne crashed . . . Chassagne badly hurt . . . and suddenly she started to cry. I never saw anyone cry like that, without sobbing—just tears running down her face, and she was white as snow. I couldn't stand it any more and so I left."

I was stroking her hand.

"Must you be a racing driver, Rudi?"

"Yes," I said. "I must."

That evening I felt that the day would come when she would be with me forever.

7

The battle on the Avus I had won, almost unconsciously, half-playfully, as one wins his victories when he is young. It was the first time that I had put myself up against drivers of international caliber—not the very greatest perhaps, but still, great drivers.

Certainly I was proud of this victory, but I was aware that such a victory meant little if one did not prove himself again ten times, a hundred times, again and again, to stay on top.

Only a few were able to do so. Most of them sank back into the anonymity of private life after a swift climb to fame, if death hadn't scooped them off the track with his bony hand. But how had those few managed it? Under what conditions did the old iron guard of the great racing drivers fight their way through, and what was the secret of their successes?

The answer to this question led straight to humility: I realized that every driver was only part of a large organism, of the firm that stood behind him. The firm created the prerequisites for victory. The highly trained brains of its engineers, the staff of mechanics drilled to precision work, the accumulated financial power in the hands of an industrial leader that could carry one across days of defeat—all these were invisible collaborators of the driver which, together, decisively determined victory or defeat.

There were four manufacturers in those days who fought

with all their power for the building of racing cars: Mercedes, Bugatti, Alfa-Romeo and Maserati. But how different were those four!

There was Bugatti, Ettore Bugatti's personal creation. He had given the firm not only his name, he had also impressed on it the mark of his own personality down to the smallest details. He bred cars as people breed horses; and he loved these cars, which he had himself designed down to the finest details, as if they were living creatures. The buildings of his little factory in Alsace looked like racing stables. One of his most successful constructions he christened the "Pur Sang," the thoroughbred. He improvised everything—his inventions, the financing of his plant which he often, and with admirable skill, steered past the cliffs of financial ruin.

One never knew exactly when he worked. Sometimes he sat for a few hours in the cabin of the big ship he had had set up in his park for his own pleasure. When he re-emerged into public view, he turned loose a rain of little slips with notes upon his construction department, the little slips containing his often ingenious spur-of-the-moment inspirations. He built racing cars because he loved them and he could only with great difficulty, and for a vast amount of money, be persuaded to sell any of them. He was anything but a businessman. For him the sport was uppermost and for that reason he loved his drivers as if they were his children. He built them a hotel of their own next to his factory so he could have them around all the time, and their victories pleased him as much as if they were his own.

Resembling him, even though not on quite the same level, were the brothers Maserati in Bologna. They were technological fanatics who sat in a tiny factory with a handful of workers and fussed around with their new constructions for months, sometimes for years. Occasionally one of the brothers entered a race himself and more often than not they and their vehicles brought home victory.

Alongside the romantics of the sport, the great concerns of Alfa and Mercedes towered gigantically. They were mammoth enterprises with thousands of workers, which took up car racing only to prove to the public the quality of their product.

Here the technician vanished behind the name of the firm. It was the business manager who bore the responsibility for the entire firm in which the construction of racing cars was only a small part.

Alfa Romeo, a large Milan firm, built—besides their racing cars—sports cars and airplane engines. But nowhere did this setup become more obvious than at Mercedes. After the merger of the Mercedes and Benz companies the new director, Dr. Kissel, had created a highly salable product and a corresponding sales organization that spanned the entire world with Mercedes dealers and was the foundation for a rapid industrial expansion of the firm itself.

Dr. Kissel took an ardent interest in the races. His technicians built a ready-for-sale sports car that could be turned into a racing car at a moment's notice by the simple expedient of detaching the fender. The technicians who designed this car remained anonymous. Whatever was created was a product of the firm and everybody had a part in it, so that it would have been unfair to stress the contribution of one particular individual. It was a trend of austere self-abnegation and modesty that ran through the entire enterprise.

I looked around among the great drivers and noticed that every one of them belonged to one of the four firms. They came from Bugatti or Alfa, from Maserati or Mercedes. They had chosen a firm, and the firm had chosen them. Because just as the good driver hankers after a good car, so a good car demanded a good driver to control it, with the ability to derive the utmost from its performance. All those ambitious men who had sold their souls to the automobile engine were young. Young and apparently of that light-hearted youthfulness that was out to conquer by storm within a few hours the fame and riches which others pursued in vain all their lives.

There was Chiron, the smiling Frenchman from the south of France. Always cheerful, always ready with a joke. Before each race he walked around his car, patted it, talked to it as to a set horse and then slid smiling behind the wheel. How many knew that behind this cheerful mask there was a hard, earnest man who denied himself almost all pleasures in life in order to be fit for the contest.

There was Nuvolari, the little, wiry man from Mantua, whom nothing could destroy. He raced an entire season with his broken leg in a plaster cast; and once, when his car burst into flames fifty meters before the finish line, he jumped out and—to the roar of the spectators—pushed the burning vehicle across the line to finish third in the race. Then there was Varzi, the elegant Milanese, seemingly soft and certainly a little too soft with regard to women and the horde of his admiring camp followers. But the same man, whose kindness was often misinterpreted and put down to weakness, was hard as steel the moment he got behind the steering wheel of his car.

There were Campari and Borzacchini, who later lost their lives in a tragic accident; blond Hans Stuck, winner of innumerable mountain races; and Manfred von Brauchitsch, my friend and teammate for many long years to come.

Then there was the old guard of Mercedes drivers: Lautenschlager, Sailer, Salzer, Werner and that powerful bear of a man, Merz. These were men who had come from the ranks of the factory and had retained the hardness, straightforwardness and simplicity of their early years. In other countries, too, many men had entered their names in the golden book of automobile racing. Many of them—most of them perhaps—are no longer with us. The machine has cost them their lives.

I am thinking of the amateur driver, Count Masetti, who was killed in the hard race of the Targa Florio; of Salamano and then Ascari, who was killed in the Grand Prix of France in Monthléry, perhaps the most famous Italian driver before Nuvolari. To this day they will show you, with awe and respect, the little house in the village where he died.

Bordino crashed in Alessandria, Italy. He collided with a dog that was crossing the track. In his memory the course was named Circuito Bordino.

Materassi, who crashed in Monza, probably was thrown off the course when another car grazed him in passing; his car killed twenty-eight persons besides himself. Arcangeli, winner of the Grand Prix of Rome, met his death while training in Monza. And there was Brilli-Peri, unforgettable with his Itala —unforgettable because of his breakneck pace and the expressions he was overheard to use while refilling his car at the pit. For reasons that were never explained, he crashed and died on the old Tripoli track.

The great Nazzaro has, like many others, retired to private life. He works for Fiat. Minoia, who drove to victory with almost all makes of cars—Benz, Mercedes, with Alfa and Bugatti—is now with Alfa Romeo. Costantini, who won the Grand Prix in style and then won the difficult Targa Florio three times, was put in charge of racing for Bugatti.

Among the Frenchmen, Wagner, Bourlier, Ballot, Goux and the public favorite, Divo, belonged to the old guard. All of them have since chosen a more peaceful profession—only Ballot was killed. Robert Benoist won many victories with Delage and Bugatti and then became sales manager at Bugatti's. Etancelin divides his life among family, business and sports. Bouriat, the very popular Bugatti driver, was killed very early in an accident.

Of the Englishmen in those years Major Seagrave used to appear on the continental race courses. Wearing green togs, he drove his green car in a number of major races but without marked success. His speed records made him famous in the automobile world. After he gave up car racing he became the victim of a speed-record attempt on the water. Sir Henry Birkin raced successfully in the Grand Prix and especially in the twenty-four-hour races—until he, too, died as a result of burns inflicted during a race. Sir Malcolm Campbell was meanwhile setting up speed records in America with a car constructed especially for him.

Those were the champion drivers of those days. They were at the height of their fame—admired and envied, but hardly any of the admirers and enviers realized that these successes, apparently won so quickly and so painlessly, had to be paid for in full, like everything else in life. Because the engine is a dangerous slave—those who are not up to it in speed of reaction and precision of brainwork, it throws pitilessly off the course. What good is the devil-may-care courage of youth, what good is devotion to the sport, if those attributes are missing?

To be a racing driver means to have the ability to be for hours on end a part of the machine—hand on wheel and on gearshift, feet on gas pedal and brake, eyes on the speedometer, the water and oil thermometer. Woe to him who, even for the fraction of a second, loses control over himself! One never allows extraneous emotions or thoughts to arise in the crucial hour of the race. The machine will crush him mercilessly. Woe to those who relinquish control over themselves to a passion, be it the passion for women, for drink or for any other addiction. They become unsure of themselves, they lose, along with self-control, mastery of the machine, and their fate is to be eliminated or to die. As in anything else in life where man aspires to great achievements—and the control over 400-horsepower is a great achievement—the goal is reached only if one's entire being is put into its service.

I believe that a person who does not have order in his private life is incapable of such service. Nor do I think that a cold technician, without passion, can achieve anything of importance in the field of car racing. Only those who can stake their entire being, who dare give themselves up wholly, can hope to win.

I myself have taken the consequences of those years when I fought my way up, step by step. I gave up the business on the Kurfuerstendamm a short time after I had opened it because one cannot, after all, serve two masters. And I submitted my life with Charly, whom I had meanwhile married, to the hard laws of my profession. She helped me during practice, she checked my time and the time of my competitors, and after the grueling months of the racing season she helped me relax.

I drove a lot in those years, and I carried home a number of victories as well as a number of defeats. Now and then I came up against a truly great driver, and whenever that happened I was forced to bring out my last reserves.

In July 1931, the Grand Prix of Germany was scheduled for the Nuerburgring. For weeks before we talked of nothing else. We knew that Bugatti had launched a new 2.3 liter car (the metric measure refers to the engine displacement) that chased over all the race courses of Europe and left every competitor behind. It was a small, very light sports car, weighing barely 700 kilo (a kilogram is about 2⅕ pounds) and the heavy Mercedes sports car SSK, with which we went into the race, weighed 2,000 kilo. Neubauer told us of the fantastic speed Chiron had got out of the little Bugatti.

Five days before the start of the race we arrived at the Nuerburgring. The cars stood in a little wood hut below the track. It was a clearing in the midst of the pines and in front of it was a meadow where we rehearsed tire changing in the evening.

"The Bugattis with their light weight probably won't need

to change tires," Neubauer said. "So we have to try not to lose the race at the pits!"

We kept changing tires—Merz, Stuck, Brauchitsch and I. My mechanic, Sebastian, and I held the record. We succeeded in changing all four tires within one minute and ten seconds. Afterward we sat together at the wooden tables under the old pine trees and discussed our chances.

"If it rains we're well off," said Merz. "But if it stays dry. . . ." He shrugged.

Yes, that was it. If the road was wet, the weight of our cars favored us. They would hold the road better and would be less likely to skid. But on a dry track the Bugattis were 1,200 kilos ahead of us, and besides, they saved at least seventy seconds which we would lose at the pits, changing tires. All told, and this we admitted only within the family, we didn't give ourselves much of a chance, even if it rained.

And then the big day came.

The weather was foggy during the early morning hours. We breakfasted in the hotel. Through the windows we could look into the street. We saw an endless parade of automobiles, bicyclists and motorcyclists winding through the town of Adenau. At least three or four thousand cars must have been heading in that direction.

The sky grew darker and darker. When we drove up to the starting line at half past nine it started to rain, a fine, gray misty rain at first, that grew heavier and heavier and finally turned into a regular downpour. Huge drops splattered on the asphalt and the wheels swooshed through the water.

There were thirty-one cars at the start. I was in the second row with Chiron next to me, and ahead of me Varzi, Fagioli and Stuck.

The flag went down—it too was heavy from the rain. The cars roared off.

I had a good start, only one ahead of me—Fagioli. I tried to pass him. But it was difficult; the rain streamed over the windshield and when I tried to peer above it a cold shower whipped painfully into my face. Fagioli's car, ahead, was throwing up a wake of water.

Finally, at the Swallow's Tail turn, I caught up with him, went past him and took the lead. I've got to gain some advantage, I thought, so that I'd have time left over to change tires.

A short glance over to the counter-straightaway showed me the entire field, the Bugattis caught in the middle. It seemed strange that they could not break out, but perhaps Chiron was holding back, planning to push ahead only in the final laps. Actually I feared him most of all, him and Varzi, because Nuvolari was driving for Alfa and the Alfas hadn't been able to accomplish much the previous year. During the third lap I got my first sign from the boxes:

CAR
FAG—48

So Fagioli in his Maserati was still at my heels. I increased my speed. The fastest tire change had taken one minute and ten seconds—I must have at least that much headstart. Again I pressed down the gas pedal. By the sixth lap my distance from the second one was one minute and two seconds. By now Nuvolari was the one behind me. It was amazing what this tough little fellow could get out of his Alfa.

During the eighth lap the rain began to let up. One could see the gray floating drifts moving eastward across the Eifel Mountains. The track was beginning to dry up. And now the Bugattis would start gaining.

There, in the tenth lap, Chiron! His name was scrawled directly under my own. He had worked his way out of the field and was now behind me in second place. There was still one minute and forty-eight seconds' distance between us, but the pits had already held up a circle, which meant that I must stop and change tires during the next round. That would cost me three-quarters of my advantage. And the roads were getting drier; the little Bugattis were running faster.

Eleventh lap. . . . We pulled up and stopped. I jumped out of the car on one side, Sebastian on the other. We tanked up, changed the tires. . . . Neubauer was standing alongside, stop watch in hand.

Ready. We were back in the car and our assistant started the motor. One minute and nine seconds. . . .

"Record time!" Neubauer called out. What else he said was drowned out by the roar of the engine. We were driving again. Nobody had caught up with us—we were still in the lead.

Twelfth lap. Signal from the boxes: Nuvolari behind me at a distance of one minute and fourteen seconds.

So Chiron had to stop, too. Probably he had to gas up. Perhaps he even had to change tires. Thank God!

Fourteenth lap. Chiron was back again, but with a distance of two minutes. I must increase speed, I mustn't let him get as close again.

In some places now the road was completely dry. Only where it ran through the woods the asphalt was still moist and shiny.

Sixteenth lap. The distance between Chiron and me had increased . . . two minutes and eight seconds now.

Eighteenth lap. Chiron was putting on speed. Our distance had shrunk to one minute and forty-five seconds.

There were four more laps to go. If Chiron held this speed he could come a lot closer to me, but he wouldn't be able to catch up with me. But what if the new Bugatti had additional untapped reserves? What if he started driving even faster?

My speedometer showed 4,000 rpm. Sebastian at my side nudged me and shook his head warningly. Never mind—I maintained my speed.

The next lap Chiron came even closer. Only one minute-and-a-half's distance between us now.

The last lap. The distance had remained unchanged—one minute and thirty seconds. Neubauer waved his flag and with the other hand signaled to slow down. I went down to 3,500 rpm. I must not ruin the engine. If only the tires held, they could never take victory away from me.

Once again around the hairpin bend behind the stands, once

again over the long, curving course that ran up the mountains, down through the valleys. . . .

There was the village of Breidscheid—there the cluster of trees marking the Hedwigshoehe; there, gleaming in the sun, the towers of the Nuerburg Castle, and there the forest of flags at the tribunes—the finish line. . . .

Brakes on—and stop. The next instant people were all over us like a sudden flood. They lifted me out of the car on their shoulders—hundreds of hands reaching out to me. The mechanics were there, the assistants to victory. Neubauer grabbed me and hugged me. And then Charly. She was standing in the back of the pit, tears running down her face.

"Rudi!" she said, her voice choked. Then we were in each other's arms. Chiron drove up and stopped right alongside me. With a graceful leap he vaulted across the hood of his car, ran toward me with his arms wide open and embraced me. Across the course, in the stands, the people were shouting "Hurrah!" and waving hats and umbrellas.

The German flag rose at the victory mast and the band struck up the national hymn. I went and got my prize.

In the evening we celebrated victory at the Adenauer Hof. Speeches, toasts, telegrams. . . . But more potent than all those external honors was the feeling of inner happiness: I've won, I've fought against the best men of the racing sport and I've carried off the prize!

Toward morning Neubauer and I stepped outside a moment to cool our wine-heavy heads. In the east it was already light, but the sun was not up yet. Between the black humps of the mountains lay the wisps of an early-morning fog.

"We must win many more such victories," I said. "This year and next year."

Neubauer looked at me. He was silent.

Finally, he spoke:

"Next year, my dear boy, Mercedes won't run any races. We're short of money. We'll have to go easy."

9

In the fall Charly and I went up to Arosa. And after a while Neubauer came to visit us there. He had retained his job but even so he was unhappy. The idea of no longer being the manager of an entire racing stable haunted him. In the evening, when we sat in our chalet in the warm glow of the lamplight, with the snow falling outside the windows, he told us his plans. Some of them were fantastic. He wanted to put together a stable of the greatest German racing drivers, take them to the States and win all available prizes there. He would sit for hours hatching plans of that sort. I liked to listen to him without being able to believe in the reality of those castles in the air. I saw, all too clearly, the facts. Auto racing was a luxury, like most things that are noble and high-born. But a poor nation could not afford luxury and we had become a poor nation.

Toward the middle of December Alfa called me—the main office in Milan. Giovannini, the racing manager of the firm, was on the phone.

"What're you doing up there, Caracciola?"

"Skiing and sun-bathing."

"Have you a contract for next year?"

"No," I said hesitantly, "not yet."

"If it's all right with you, I'll come up to see you toward the end of the month."

"All right," I said and hung up.

He arrived in Arosa the last day of the year. Giovannini was a small, elegant man with blondish hair and shining brown eyes. With typical southern temperament he embraced me, slapped me on the shoulder and kissed both of Charly's hands.

When he spotted Neubauer he flinched. The two knew each other from many races where Mercedes and Alfa had competed. As we went in to dinner, he whispered to me excitedly:

"What's the matter? Is Mercedes going to race again after all?"

I shrugged.

Thanks to Neubauer's volubility dinner was quite lively. He and Giovannini kept measuring each other with searching glances. Right after dinner Giovannini said:

"There's something I'd like to discuss with you, Signor Caracciola, but in private, please."

We went into my study. Neubauer and my wife remained at the table.

When we were alone, Giovannini, without another word, reached into his breast pocket. He had brought the contract along, all filled in; all I had to do was to sign it. I lit the two candles on the desk and read through the contract. It was a decent offer—a small guarantee, the entire starting bonus and half the prizes for me. Only one point made me hesitate. It was a provision that I was to start outside the Alfa team.

"Why that?" I asked, turning around to look at Giovannini. He was standing behind me and looking over my shoulder as he read.

"I don't know," he said reluctantly. Obviously my question embarrassed him. "You know, all our drivers work on a participation basis—and since you aren't as familiar with our cars . . . you know, it's an entirely different thing to drive a heavy Mercedes or one of those little Monopostos . . . perhaps our boys thought that you wouldn't get used to our small cars right away. . . ."

"Oh? And who thought that?"

"I don't know."

"Nuvolari?"

"No."

"Borzacchini?"

"No, not he either."

"Well, then, Campari?"

He waved me off. "Stop asking these questions, please."

So then it was Campari. I might have known. But could I really object to that? I myself didn't know whether I'd get used to the new cars.

I left the contract on the desk and went to the dining room to get some wine and cigars. When I turned back, Neubauer came after me and caught me in the hall.

"Rudi!" he said, grabbing my lapels. "Rudi, you're not going to go over to the other side, are you?"

I felt almost sorry for him at that moment.

"But I've got to drive, don't you see?" I said.

He didn't reply but he still held on to me. It was a strange moment, the two of us standing in the dimly lit hall and in both of us the vivid memory of eight battle-filled years together. At that moment Neubauer was closer to me than a brother. He took a deep breath and said:

"Promise me one thing, Rudi—if Mercedes ever races again, you'll come back to us."

"Yes," I said and shook his hand.

He turned on his heel and went back to Charly. I looked after him as he went through the bright door, broad-shouldered and with head bowed. Then the door closed and I remained standing, staring at it. And I felt as if something had left me irrevocably, something very beautiful—perhaps it was youth, perhaps it was the memory of those years of aspiration. I could not put it into words.

Then I went back to Giovannini and signed the contract with Alfa.

Two months later I went down to Milan, to my new firm, for the first time. Giovannini received me and introduced me to the big shots. Director General Gianferrari, a very correct gentleman, greeted me with formal politeness.

"I hope you will enjoy yourself with us," he said, giving me a slim, brown hand. Then we went over to Jano, the chief designer, who sat in a cloud of cigarette smoke staring at his blueprints. He greeted me vivaciously and took me down to the factory's testing lab. Here he introduced me to the mechanics. One of them, named Bonini, was assigned to me —a fresh-faced, brown-skinned boy who had worked in Germany for two years and spoke almost fluent German. We chatted a little and found that we liked each other quite a lot.

Then Jano showed me his newest model. It was a graceful, racy one-seater, lightweight and easy to maneuver. I liked it at first sight. The next day we drove to Monza. Jano wanted my opinion of the new car. Driving it was totally different compared to my heavy SSK Mercedes. I drove without effort but I had to watch like a hawk in order to keep the fast little car under control.

"Well, how did she go?" Jano asked when I climbed out.

"As light-footed as a ballerina," I said.

Jano laughed. "I think you and I understand each other," he said, sounding pleased and holding out his hand.

He was right. I came to rely on him a great deal and he never let me down.

The following day I returned to Arosa and a week later I came back to enter the Mille Miglia race. A year earlier I had won that race with Mercedes, but I thought I had a good chance this time, too. However, it didn't turn out that way. I was first in Rome, but then a valve connection broke and I had to drop out in Verona, unable to even gain a place.

I can still see the expression on Campari's face when I arrived back at the factory. He smiled to himself as if to say, Well, didn't I tell you that one wasn't going to make it?

The next race was in Monte Carlo. Again the entire Alfa team was there and I participated. It was a very difficult race. Nuvolari took the lead from the start. He put on a speed that was almost murderous on the long, tortuous course. I had gotten off to a bad start and was in the middle of the field, but with each lap I worked my way forward until, finally, I was second in line behind Nuvolari.

There is an unwritten rule among drivers of the same caliber: if two from the same team are ahead they are not to compete with each other, but the one who had the lead until the first half time was to drive home to victory. The rule exists for the benefit of the firm for which the driver starts, because if the second man forces the pace too much there is the danger of over-straining the engines and both cars may fail, making the company the real loser.

The rule is a time-honored one and professional drivers consider it etiquette to stick to it. However, young, ambitious drivers often violate it.

I was following Nuvolari's red car and noticed that, with each second, I was coming closer. During the last lap I was so close that I could look into his car. He had slowed down considerably and we were driving side by side, almost wheel to wheel. I saw him shifting with nervous, hasty gestures. Apparently his fuel line was fouled, or else he had to switch over to the reserve tank.

I thought quickly: I was not part of the team. They had rejected me. I had no obligations toward the Alfa people. If I got Nuvolari now no one could reproach me. Of course, it would be fairer if I let him keep the lead. I slowed down. While driving by I glanced at the stands. The people were jumping to their feet and shouting. Then came the finish line. Nuvolari drove through first with me following right behind. When I got out of my car there were jeers and whistles of contempt from the spectators. They felt betrayed, assuming that I had made a deal with Nuvolari. I left the car and went over to the pits. My mechanic came toward me.

"Why did you do that, Signor Caracciola?" he asked.

"I don't know," I said. I felt miserable. After all, it was the first time the public had hailed me with jeers. Then I saw Giovannini coming toward me, holding out both arms.

"That was decent of you, Caracciola," he said. "That was really decent. And I'm to ask you, on behalf of the others, whether you'd like to be a member of the team."

"And Campari?" I asked.

"He wants you too; he wants you to very much."

Thus I became a member of the Alfa team.

It was a good year for the firm. The little Monoposto took all the big prizes. Nuvolari got the Grand Prix of France and Italy and I the Grand Prix of Germany and Monza, not counting the lesser victories.

It was indeed a blessed year for Alfa. If the firm continued like this in the winter, we could look hopefully to the future.

When the season was over, we separated and Charly and I went back up into the mountains, to Arosa. It was a magnificent winter. The days were blue and gold. Without a blemish to mar its purity the great wide sky stretched above us. We had been there two weeks when I received a letter from the firm. They were giving me notice.

They were going to give up building racing cars; it was too costly, they wrote, and the expense did not justify the results. In closing they advised me to join the Scuderia Ferrari. Signor Ferrari was going to take over the existing stable of cars and would continue the business at his own expense.

At that time Chiron was in Arosa. He had a similar letter from Bugatti in his pocket and he, like myself, was unemployed.

We often met skiing and in the evening we sometimes sat together at our house, sometimes at the hotel where he was staying and occasionally in one of the ski huts up in the mountains. He was a great fellow, clean inside and out, and a good friend.

"You know, Rudi," he said one evening, "why should we always get the prizes for other people? It would be much smarter to start our own firm."

He had already thought everything out, including the name. The company was to be called Scuderia C.C. (Caracciola-Chiron). Excitedly he drew up a financial prospectus of the new firm on a slip of paper.

On the profit side there were the money prizes, the starting premiums and the advertising subsidies of the various factories. On the expense side there were only the costs of the cars to be bought, the transport and traveling expenses and the wages for two mechanics.

His plan seemed a good one to me. Our names were known in all countries. Each of us had a long list of victories to show. As competitors we had fought each other in a sporting way and as friends we got along excellently. The factories no longer entered races; Chiron and I were unemployed; and thus the Scuderia C.C. came into being.

We bought two racing cars from Alfa-Romeo and the Daimler Benz people generously put a diesel truck at our disposal for conveying them. For a long time we discussed the color of the two cars. I can still see them, the enormous, light-gray truck and the two racy-looking cars—Chiron's blue with white stripes, and mine white with blue stripes. The doors of the truck were adorned with the beautifully ornamented letters of our firm's monogram: C.C.

One shadow fell across the bright hope of this promising beginning. Bonini, my mechanic, could no longer work. He had suffered bad burns in a factory accident and was in the hospital. So I had to try to get along without my faithful helper and hire another mechanic from Alfa-Romeo.

10

The first race which the Scuderia C.C. entered was the Grand Prix of Monaco. It was to be run in Monte Carlo. We drove down to Monte a week before the race.

Since Chiron had never driven an Alfa, we practiced especially long and thoroughly. Twenty-five times we chased around the merry-go-round, down the winding road to the sea along the short straightaway along the shore and then back up the winding road to the summit of the course. I increased my speed with each lap. In the rear-view mirror I could see that Chiron was always close behind me. His talent was astonishing. Within a moment he had got used to the new car and handled it as if he had been driving it for years.

When I raced downhill on the twenty-fifth lap I suddenly did not see Chiron anymore. I wanted to slow down. I braked, but the brake did not hold. It blocked only one front wheel and the car skidded toward the stone parapet that separated the curve from the precipice. I steered against it, I tried to shift gears . . . the curve came swiftly closer. I was aware that I could not make the curve at over 80 and I was going at 100 kilometers per hour, perhaps even faster. I held to the right where the stone wall reared steeply up. It was better to crash against the stone than to fall over the parapet into the sea below. The wall raced toward me—I crashed against it, metal against stone . . . the car stood still.

Nothing had happened. Only the body of the car was smashed, especially around my seat. Carefully I drew my leg out of the steel trap. Bracing myself against the frame of the body, I slowly extricated myself from the seat.

Behind me an ear-splitting screech . . . the brakes of Chiron's car. I looked around. He stopped just behind me and jumped out of the car. Other people came running down the stone steps.

I tried to hurry out of the car. I wanted to show that nothing had happened to me, that I was absolutely unhurt.

I stepped to the ground. At that instant the pain flashed through my leg. It was a ferocious pain, as if my leg were being slashed by hot, glowing knives. I collapsed, Chiron catching me in his arms. Then the others arrived, some of them helping to support me.

Two persons ran into a small tobacco shop a little farther up the road. They came back with a chair, put me on that chair and carried me up the street into the shop. Inside it was cool and dim. They set the chair carefully on the ground and someone pushed a carton under my foot so that I could stretch my leg.

Behind the counter stood an old man with a white goatee, wearing a black velvet cap. He looked at me half shocked, half curious, and said with a set smile, as if he were making a sale: "Do make yourself comfortable, monsieur; the ambulance will arrive presently. We have an excellent hospital." He went on consolingly, "Some of the most famous people have died there."

It took a long time for the ambulance to arrive. I sat on my chair and suffered the most dreadful pains. People were standing all around me, others were staring through the door into the shop. I was afraid someone would notify Charly and she would rush down to the shop. But luckily the ambulance got there first.

They put me on a stretcher and shoved me inside the car like a bread into the oven. Inside the ambulance it was narrow and hot. It smelled of carbolic and it was impossible to look out through the milk-white glass panes.

The drive seemed endless. Once the ambulance rattled across cobblestones and I could feel each jolt go through me, from my toes to the roots of my hair.

Finally we stopped. I was lifted out on the stretcher and put on the ground. I found myself in a large park beneath great, ancient plane trees. Then two ambulance men grabbed the stretcher and carried me across the crunching gravel through a red brick portal into the hospital.

At first they took me into the X-ray lab and from there into surgery. They laid me down on a white-sheeted table and through the upper part of the windows I could see a piece of blue sky and a few treetops that were moving in the wind.

A young man in a white smock glanced down at me and then started to rattle around with gleaming instruments on a glass table. A nurse pushed her coif through the door and asked:

"Is that the racer with the broken leg?"

"Yes, this is the fracture," said the young doctor.

"Dr. Trentini will be here in five minutes," said the nurse and closed the door with a bang.

I just lay there feeling the most awful pains. At first it hadn't been half as bad as now. Apparently the shock had numbed the nerves then, but now I had a feeling as if someone were sawing away at my bones without letup.

Then Dr. Trentini arrived. He was a small man with a lemon-yellow face and a little black goatee. He introduced himself and also his assistant, whose name was Porrati. Both bowed.

I just lay there in pain. If they'd only get going, I thought.

A nurse arrived with the X-ray picture. Both doctors went to the window, held the X-ray against the light and explained something to each other in whispering voices. I tried to hear what they said but I couldn't understand a thing.

They came back to the table on which I was lying and Dr. Trentini took my leg by the heel and started to pull at it.

"Does it hurt?" he asked.

"Yes," I said through clenched teeth. "But the leg must not be shortened, Doctor, do you understand? Pull as much as you want."

The assistant took over. He was younger and stronger and pulled even harder. Sweat broke through every pore of my body. While the assistant pulled, Dr. Trentini dragged up a bucket and took from it a white bandage. A milky-looking liquid was dripping from the bandage.

"Plaster," said Dr. Trentini, smiling kindly at me. Then he started to unroll the bandage. He put it directly on the skin without putting on a stocking first. The bandage was cold and slippery and Dr. Trentini was breathing noisily.

The door to the hall was opened and I heard Charly's voice outside:

"Where is my husband? Can't I see my husband?"

The door was closed again and the nurse, who had come in, said:

"Doctor, there is a lady outside who wants to talk to you."

Dr. Trentini dropped the bandage on the spot. He washed his hands and went out. I saw him taking the X-ray along.

He stayed outside for a very long time and at one point I thought I could hear Charly weeping.

Much later I learned what he told Charly outside the operating room. He had shown her the X-ray and said:

"Look at that, madame; the thigh and the entire tibular bone are completely mashed. Your husband will never be able to drive again."

I knew nothing of all that. I was only lying flat on the operating table, my head pressed against the hard pillow, my nails dug deep into the flesh and praying: Dear God, let this be over soon!

11

The little doctor with the lemon-yellow face was standing at the foot of the bed.

"And when can I get up again?" I asked.

He shrugged his shoulders.

"Do you think this thing will come out all right?"

He shrugged again, took the stethoscope out of the breast pocket of his white jacket, regarded it pensively, put it back in his pocket.

"Perhaps," he said. "We'll have to wait and see. Perhaps nature will help itself, and if not—there's always the operation as a last resort."

He gave a polite little bow and went to the door. He walked very straight with a somewhat bouncing stride, like a bird. Small, vain people often walk that way.

"But then I won't be able to drive again?" I almost shouted.

He turned around; he smiled. "Oh, no, I wouldn't say that. There are miracles. . . ."

He waved and the door fell shut behind him. I was alone. I lay there as if someone had struck me a blow on the head. So that was it! They were going to experiment a little more and then they would operate. And this little lemon-yellow person talked about it as if it were merely a matter of taking off my stocking.

Toward noon Giovannini came to visit me. He was very cheerful, or at least he acted that way.

"Well, Rudi, rear axle damaged, eh? So what; it'll be straightened out again. Brought along a bottle of machine oil." He reached into his pocket that bulged with a big, pot-bellied shape at his hip and brought forth a bottle of brandy.

I shook my head. "I don't feel like drinking. They want to put a saw to my leg."

"What?" His jaw dropped. But then he started talking so fast that his words tumbled over one another.

Under no circumstances must they do that. Out of the question. Only one man could help me: Professor Putti from Bologna. He was going to send for Putti, if necessary have him come at his own, Giovannini's, expense. And then we'd see! He said good-by and nearly ran out of the room.

Putti arrived the following morning. I liked him the moment he came in. A tall, slender man with a sharp brown face and snow-white hair. He introduced himself and started examining my leg right away. The doctor with the lemon-yellow face and his two assistants stood behind him and watched him with offended expressions.

Putti examined me at length and very thoroughly. When he was finished he straightened up without saying a word.

"Must I have an operation?" I asked fearfully.

"Who said you did?"

I motioned with my head toward the little doctor. Putti turned around and looked at him, but said nothing. I could only see the little doctor's face. It had turned even yellower; he bit his lip so hard that his black mustache trembled.

Then Putti turned to me, held out his hand, and said:

"Don't worry, Mr. Caracciola, it'll be all right. But it would be better if you came to me at my clinic at Bologna. I'll discuss the necessary steps with Dr. Trentini."

He shook my hand and smiled. His snow-white teeth stood out sharply in his tanned face.

Then he left, the three other doctors trotting after him. I remained lying there, waiting to be brought to Bologna. My pains were terrible. The formless plaster cast closed around me like a stone corset, pressing and pinching everywhere. I was thinking that the race on Sunday would take place without me now and I was very unhappy. I looked around me, at the ocean of flowers whose fragrance filled the little room. Then I thought of the race again, ceaselessly, for many, many hours.

On Monday I was carried to a car and transported to Bologna. Just before Genoa we encountered my mechanics. They were taking my damaged car to the factory. We stopped and said hello. It was a distressing reunion; my car was just as sick as I was. Then we went on, each to a different destination. I painfully raised my head and looked after them until they vanished in a cloud of dust under the gray olive trees. I felt as if my own youth, my happy past, filled with conflict and adventure, had passed me by just then, never to return.

The hospital at Bologna was an ancient convent, spacious, quiet and cool. I was in a room facing on the garden. I heard the birds sing, saw the sunshine wander across the lawn and disappear into the lengthening evening shadows. Day after day. Time stood still. You could hear the wind rustling in the treetops.

Charly was with me all day long. We played cards and sometimes we talked about how it would be when I could walk again. When there was a road race somewhere, we clung to the radio. Things weren't going well with the Scuderia C.C. Chiron had begun to hit a streak of bad luck. Every race he entered, he lost. At the Grand Prix of France he had tire trouble, on the Nuerburgring he dropped out during the second lap. We put all our hopes on the Avus race in Berlin.

Practice was broadcast by the Berlin radio. I had my headphones clamped on and lived on the road with them, just as in 1926. Suddenly I felt as if I'd been struck a blow in the chest. The announcer, who had been gushing words, broke off; then another, muffled, throaty voice said:

"We have just received information that Mercedes-Benz

driver Merz has skidded off the course; he is said to be badly injured." After a pause, the same muffled voice announced: "Otto Merz is dead."

Another great one, another of the grand old guard. What a man he had been! What a man, with the heart of a child. He was so strong that he could lift a racing car by himself while they put on fresh tires; and I with my own eyes saw him drive a nail through a two-inch wooden table top with a blow of his fist. He always laughed when they talked about the dangers of road racing and said he felt sorry for the milestone that his head would crack one day. And now he had been carried out of the curve into the great darkness.

That Sunday Chiron lost again. But I hardly paid attention, I was too shaken by Merz's death.

Professor Putti came to see me every day. He'd enter my room with the brisk cheerfulness of a busy doctor, look good-humoredly at my leg that lay like a dead tree trunk in its plaster, and say, "Well, it'll be all right. . . ." and disappear again, his white gown waving like a flag behind him.

Five months it went like that, day after day. Then one day the head physician came in with two nurses. They removed the plaster cast, lifted me on a stretcher and rolled me over to the X-ray lab. I was photographed from every side, then they took me back to my bed. In the evening Putti arrived, announcing cheerfully:

"Now another month in the cast and then we'll be all right."

I clenched my teeth and was silent. What could I say? Another month in the cast—he said it as if it were a joke. But I was lying there, buried alive. The engines roared, the cars raced over the white strip of road in Germany, in Italy, in France. But I was no longer with them.

Four days later Putti sailed off to America, to participate in a conference. The head physician took over.

Four weeks later the plaster was taken off again. I was allowed to get up. Supported by two crutches I tried painfully to walk, but I couldn't. I clenched my teeth. The next day a nurse pushed me in a wheel chair through the dimly lit hall of the hospital.

When you are healthy you never think of all the pain and suffering in the world, and I was shocked at the procession of misery that was passing me here: men and women on crutches and in wheel chairs, with rattling artificial limbs or with white-bandaged arm stumps. They emerged from the shadows, passed me in silence and disappeared again in the dim archways of the old convent.

A couple of days earlier I had heard, from the nurse, that Giovannini, too, had entered the hospital. Uremic poisoning. A hopeless case the nurse had said.

After a few days I hobbled over to him on my crutches. He was in a small, dark room, probably a former penitentiary cell, and he was alone. His hands were folded on his chest he was staring at the ceiling. I sat down next to the bed. He said nothing when I came in; only his eyes had greeted me. I wanted to cheer him up.

"Well, old pal," I said. "They really got the two of us, didn't they? I guess this season the others will have to do without us."

He shook his head slowly and painfully.

"This is the end of me, Rudi."

He could only whisper hoarsely. His voice was gone; he was too weak. Then he pushed back his cover and showed me his legs—formless and swollen, they helplessly hung from his emaciated body.

"Water. It rises and rises and when it reaches here"—he pointed to his heart— "then everything is over."

He pulled his cover up again and lay there without moving. His eyes were closed.

"Can I do anything for you?" I asked.

His eyelids fluttered, then he rose on his elbow and said, straining and panting:

"Yes, you can do something for me. You can tell the doctor to give me something so I can croak at last. Enough morphine to help me across."

He let himself drop back to the pillow and closed his eyes. He looked as if he were already dead.

I left silently. Outside, Charly was waiting and she and the nurse brought me back to my room. The following day I didn't go back to Giovannini.

12

Now, you'll see, from now on it'll be a little better every day," said Charly. She was smiling with tears in her eyes.

On the third day they X-rayed me again. The head physician and the X-ray technician were present. They did not comment.

In the evening the doctor came in carrying a large envelope containing the X-ray of my leg.

"You see—here"—he pointed to a place on the X-ray. "The cartilage at the point of fracture has shifted."

"And what does that mean?"

"The leg isn't ready to support your weight yet," he said. "It would be best to operate. We could put in a screw to fasten the fracture."

I shook my head.

"Then you'll have to go back into plaster," he said firmly. "For at least a month."

"No."

"All right, then you'll have to bear the consequences. Under these circumstances I must withdraw from any further treatment."

He went out. In the door he turned back once more.

"But do be reasonable, Mr. Caracciola. There is no other choice. Either you wait until the cartilage has hardened and the bone can carry you again—in which case we'll have to put the leg back into plaster today—or you submit to an operation."

I said nothing and looked at Charly. She was standing at the head of my bed, her hands clenched around the brass rails so that the knuckles stood out white. She was crying silently.

The doctor was still waiting for an answer. At last he bowed stiffly and left.

"Let them operate, Rudi," Charly burst out. She was weeping aloud now, her entire body was shaking with sobs.

"And what if the joint remains stiff? What if I can't drive again?"

"You won't be able to drive anyhow!"

"What—what are you saying?"

She looked at me aghast. Then she repeated, almost stubbornly, "No, you can't drive again. The doctor told me—the thigh—the neck of the femur, he called it—is completely smashed."

"Who said so?"

"Dr. Trentini—"

I felt my body growing utterly stiff with shock. An icy cold crept from my heart into all my limbs.

Charly sat down on my bed and reached for my hand.

"Shouldn't I have told you?"

"Yes—oh, yes."

She was silent. Everything inside me rebelled against this senseless cruelty of fate. No, that couldn't, that must not be!

"But must you drive? Couldn't you start something else? There are so many things to do."

"Please, stop it."

Oh, she could not understand what it meant to me—the roar of the engines starting, the high whine of the supercharger and the swift flight along the bright road. This intoxication of speed, the hardest, coldest and yet the most beautiful intoxication fate can give a man! She was glad when I sat with her, safe in the lamplight and happy with her in her fashion. I had hurt her—I felt sorry for her.

I pressed her hand.

"I'll try it just once more. Tonight I'll talk to the X-ray man. If he feels the same way as the head doctor, I'll go back into the cast tomorrow."

In the evening I asked to see the X-ray man. He confirmed the diagnosis of his superior in all points. The next morning my leg was put back into plaster.

Two days later Giovannini died, and three weeks afterward, Professor Putti returned from America.

He and I had a long talk. I told him quite frankly what I thought: that I had lost all faith in the science of medicine and trusted only in my own healthy constitution. He smiled.

"There are three things, Signor Caracciola," he said, "which can make a sick man healthy again: faith, will power and the doctors. And I won't insist that the doctors are the greatest force of the three."

I pressed his hand. I liked him enormously. He stood above his vocation and regarded it with cheerful skepticism; perhaps he was a great doctor for that very reason.

Two weeks later I was released from the hospital. I walked on two crutches and the smashed leg hurt dreadfully with each step. With Charly I went up to Lugano where friends of mine had a house. Lugano is warm and sunny. And I needed warmth and sun for my sick leg.

The house of our friends was close to the lake. All day I sat on the terrace and looked out on the water. The mountains were mirrored in it and clouds moved across it—it was a continuous interplay of light and shadow and I never got tired of watching it.

In the middle of November Mercedes called—Neubauer asking how I felt and whether I was going to drive again next season.

"Yes," I said.

"Great, great!" he said, and asked whether it would be all right with me if he came over the following weekend.

"But of course," I said, "by all means."

I spent the days until Saturday in growing excitement. Mercedes had called. That meant Mercedes was going to build racing cars again. That meant they wanted me to drive for them again.

I harassed the doctor in Lugano with my requests for thinner, less obtrusive bandages. With Charly's help I forced a pair of trousers over the injured leg, and in front of the mirror I rehearsed steps as in an actor's studio. Nobody was to notice how much walking still hurt me.

Then Saturday arrived. Charly picked up Neubauer at the train while I stayed home and waited. Then I heard them drive up in front of the house. Heavy steps came thundering up the stairs. The door opened and Neubauer came toward me, his arms wide open. I got up and limped a few steps toward him. He pulled me to him, slapped me on the back and said cheerfully:

"Rudi, good old Rudi! How wonderful, how good to see you back on your feet again!"

He beamed all over his face, but his dark eyes were studying me intently and at length. We sat down.

"Well, then," he started, "you may have guessed by now: we're building again. Things are looking up in Germany and the German firms are making racing cars once more!" He put his heavy hand on my knee—it was rather painful, but I didn't flinch. "And how about you, Rudi? Would you like to? Can you drive again?"

"Of course I can," I said calmly. "And I'd like to, yes. But it depends on the kind of contract you offer."

His eyebrows rose in astonishment.

Since I thought he might have a contract in his pocket, I continued by asking outright exactly what kind of contract the firm had in mind. But he waved off with both hands.

"Really, Rudi, I don't know. You'd have to come to Stuttgart yourself and discuss this with Dr. Kissel. I actually came merely as a friend, in order to spend a few happy hours with you."

We spent a few "happy hours." My leg hurt awfully; the plaster cast seemed to have loosened and I had the unpleasant feeling that Neubauer was following each step I took with his eyes in order to determine how well my "rear axle" was working back into shape. On the following day he went back to Stuttgart and reported:

"Caracciola is still in bad shape, we can't count on him for the time being."

I couldn't get angry when I heard about it. I knew the business. Neubauer had only acted in the interests of the firm. And a businessman is not allowed sentiments. Persons can have merely a functional importance for him. Once a man can no longer fulfill this function, he has to go. It is a hard law, as pitiless as the battle for existence and survival in nature. But it is valid without exception for all men who have devoted themselves to the Machine.

In January I went to Stuttgart and signed my contract. It was a contract I would not have accepted a year earlier. But now I was stretched out on my bed in a hotel room, unable to get up because the trip had strained my leg so, and so I signed. I signed without resentment, in fact with a certain amount of gratitude. After all, all things considered I had to be grateful that they were giving me another chance.

Afterward I went to Arosa with Charly. "Sun, sun, sun!" the doctor we had consulted in Stuttgart had advised.

And up there was sun indeed. It shone the whole day, from a steel-blue sky and reflected a thousandfold from a glittering snowscape. We had rented a little house where we lived alone. I spent all day lying on the balcony while Charly took care of the household. It was as in the first days of our love. Usually we talked of our hopes and how it would be when I could drive again. Every evening we went out together, a little farther each time. I'd put an arm around her shoulder, supporting myself with a cane on the other side. I didn't want to go out during the day—no one must see me during my walking exercises.

I knew how much Charly loved to ski. After the long months of voluntary prison in Bologna she would love the idea of making a long ski tour with some friends of ours. At first she said no, but finally I talked her into it.

So one morning she took off for an especially beautiful tour. We had agreed that I was to pick her up at the station in the afternoon. Toward five I went down to the station. The train arrived but she was not on it. Nor was anyone else of that tour. I was disappointed and limped back up to our little house. I sat at the window, waiting. The evening light crept higher and higher up the mountains, and gradually it faded and blue shadows rose from the valleys. I did not turn on the light. It was very dark in the room and I watched the first stars appear and the boat-shaped moon swimming up over the mountains from the east.

At seven there was a call from Lenzerheide, one of the Alpine stations. The telephone operator told me the party wanted me to know they would not return until the last train. There had been an accident and that had held them up.

"What kind of accident . . . ?"

She didn't know.

The last train arrived at half past nine. From the window in the bedroom I could look down to the station. I saw the train with its brightly lit windows come climbing up the mountain. Then it stopped. The bright white of the square outside the station turned dark with people.

I lit the candles and went back into the dining room. It was now a quarter of ten. I opened the window and looked out. Cold night air came streaming in and the candles started to flicker.

A skier came walking up the road, the skis on his shoulder. The snow crunched under his boots. I saw him from afar and thought at first that it was Charly. But when the figure came nearer, I saw that it was a man. When he reached our house, he took down his skis and leaned them against a lamppost. Then he came toward the entrance door.

I closed the window, took a candle and walked out quickly as I could. When I came out in the stairway, there was a knock on the door downstairs.

"Come on up, won't you!" I called. My voice sounded strange even to myself.

The door opened and the man came upstairs. I lifted the candle to light his way. He was a young man who had been one of the members of the tour.

"Good evening, Mr. Caracciola," he said.

"Good evening."

"I wanted—"

Suddenly he stopped and looked at me. The light of the candle fell directly on his face. I saw his eyes and I knew everything.

"Charly?" I asked. He nodded.

"Dead?" I forced the word out of a dry throat. He nodded. I reached for the banister. We stood facing each other in silence. The stairway was dark; the candle flickered in my hand. In the light of the candle his face looked lifeless, like a death mask. He began to speak:

"The avalanche came toward her . . . she must have seen it. She keeled over, right into the avalanche—probably a heart attack."

Then we were facing each other silently again. Suddenly he turned on his heel, ran down the stairs. He ran as if someone were chasing him. Downstairs he slammed the door behind him.

I went back into the dining room and extinguished the candles —all except the one I held in my hand.

13

One day Chiron came to see me, unannounced. I was lying on a couch in a darkened room. I hadn't expected him—not him or anyone else.

He threw his coat over a chair and sat down across from me. He didn't offer his condolences and I was grateful for that.

"*Bon jour*, Rudi," he said. He talked lightly, as if we had separated only the night before. "Wouldn't you like to drive the lap of honor? down in Monte? They were going to write you, Noghès told me. But I said, 'Ah, bah, why write! I'll go to Arosa and bring him right down with me.'"

"No," I said. "I'd rather not."

He got up and came over to me. He put both hands on my shoulders.

"But Rudi, you've got to get out of this cave sometime. You're still a young man, you can't retire just yet!"

He talked to me for half an hour. Finally I said yes.

On the day of the race I didn't arrive in Monte Carlo till one o'clock. The race started at three o'clock. It was a magnificent spring day. The white roads of the town shimmered in the sunlight and the sea stretched its warm blue to the horizon. I didn't go to the grid till just before the race. When I drove past the stands a young girl handed a bouquet of roses into my car. The president got up and waved. Among the spectators, too, many rose and greeted me.

I drove very slowly past the pit. The cars were standing at the pit, being readied by the mechanics. The starting roar of the engines carried all the way over to me.

In the side streets people waved and cheered. There was the fateful curve and there the stone steps where I had smashed my leg.

I drove on, a stretch along the seaside where I could hear the waves splash against the rocks and feel a fresh breeze rising up from the water. It was good racing weather.

I drove on. The right leg began to hurt, I had to work both gas pedal and brake with the left foot. When I returned to the start the cars had already drawn up. They stood four rows deep, the red Italians and the blue Frenchmen. I stopped, got out, and looked over to the field. I knew them all, all those who were at the start.

There was Nuvolari's small, wiry toreador's figure and there Chiron, France's most successful champion, in his light-blue racing suit with his red-and-white dotted scarf. There, Varzi with his precisely parted hair and his eternally smoldering cigarette; and Earl Howe, the senior of the English amateur drivers with his shrewdly smiling eyes, this time without his gray umbrella. Next to Earl Howe's shiny, polished Bugatti stood Moll, the rising young French driver, and "Fifi" Etancelin. I saw Dreyfus, who had already won Monte Carlo once; and Faroux, the starter, the greatest pro of the French automobile reporters. He was famous throughout the world for his objective accounts of road races; a gentleman all the way.

Faroux raised the flag—the motors howled, a reek of castor-oil fumes wafted over to me. The flag came down, and they were off. I watched them—a howling pack—disappear in a cloud. Then I turned around and, past the stands, went out.

Returning to the race course had shaken me more than I had thought. That was my world, that's where I belonged. A man is a racing driver as another is a hunter. From instinct, from an urge that originates deeper than conscious thought. I had always had contempt for the others, for the boys who sat at the steering wheel only to hunt down retirement pay. You are a racing driver because it is your fate, or you will never be one.

I had to drive again. It was the only way to endure life. But what would become of me if I tried and then failed? The leg had been hurting me already, today, on this short drive. How could I last in a race of three, four, five hundred kilometers? But even so—I had to drive again if I was to bear life at all. But what if I drove again and could not compete with the young and the hale? They would rub salt into my wounds. I knew it all: Caracciola has not regained his old form . . . too old . . . there are no comebacks in sports. . . .

But for me there had to be a comeback. I had to be master of my body. Otherwise life was pointless.

Because—what else would I do? Become a businessman again, just a businessman selling cars? That was a way out for those, perhaps, who raced for money. But for me racing was more. Let there be people who smiled or shrugged at the idea of men risking their lives to be a few seconds faster than others. For me the only happiness was to sit in the car, crouched behind the windshield waiting for the starter to lower the flag, and then to speed off, perhaps a fraction of a second faster than the rest. . . .

And then those hours on the road: the wind whistles by and the motors roar, and there is a roaring inside you because you are no longer a man with a bad leg and a sad heart, but you are master over three hundred—four hundred horses. You are the will that controls this creature of steel; you think for it, you are in tune with its rhythm. And your brain works with the same speed and precision as this heart of steel. Or else the monster turns master over you and destroys you. I had to drive. There was nothing else for me.

No! There was no way back. I had to drive again—I had to, had to, had to!

Two weeks later came a telegram from Mercedes: practice on

the Avus was about to begin. The new model—34—was to be tested.

I went to Berlin. I arrived in the evening at the hotel where Neubauer and Dr. Niebel, the designer of the car, were expecting me.

I was still walking with a cane. Neubauer was scrutinizing me. They had been there for two days and had already started practicing with Brauchitsch and Fagioli. They had broken in the new car. It was making passable time, nothing sensational yet. I was to start the next morning at eleven. I asked if I couldn't start earlier—I didn't want to make a press sensation with my first start. I saw Neubauer and Niebel exchanging a quick look. Then Neubauer said:

"But, of course, Caracciola—whatever you wish."

So we met the following morning out on the Avus.

When I arrived the others were already there—Neubauer, Niebel and the mechanics. The car was there, too, small and white. It looked very racy, the kind of one-seater I had always dreamed of driving.

It was a lovely May morning. The sky was light blue. The sun shone down on the tops of the pines and there was a warm, resinous smell around us.

I drove my car close to the racer, got out, and went over on my cane. The mechanics helped me get into the seat. I felt my heart pounding in my throat.

A young man with a notebook and pencil approached me, but Neubauer held him back. A press photographer's camera snapped. A mechanic started the motor and jumped back. I drove off. The first lap I drove carefully, feeling my way. The leg hurt a little, but it was bearable.

I stepped down a little harder. The car developed speed. The woods to the right and left melted into a gray-green wall. The white band of the road seemed to narrow and the whistling wind rose to a high whine.

Thank God, we were doing fine! I could still drive!

After the seventh lap came the stop sign from the pits. After the eighth I quit. Neubauer and Niebel came over to me.

"Well, how was it?"

"Quite all right, Dr. Niebel," I said. "I'm quite satisfied with the engine, but we could do better at the curves if the road was laid out properly."

Niebel didn't look very pleased. Neubauer said nothing. The mechanics helped me out of the car and I went back to my own car, trying to lean as little as possible on the cane and not to let the leg drag. I would have liked to ask how I had made out, but I didn't want to lose face.

The young man with the notebook, whom Neubauer had previously held back, now rushed up to me, murmuring a name I didn't catch. I looked at him. He was pale, had blond hair which he wore combed back, and his eyes peered from behind rimless pince-nez. His manner was that of a nervous, hunted animal.

"Congratulations, Mr. Caracciola," he said. "You did splendidly."

"Oh?" I said in a most indifferent tone, while my heart was beating faster.

"You did 235 on the last lap," said the young man. "Better time than they did yesterday in practice."

"Well, that's good," I said. I could have hugged the man.

"And how about that?" he pointed with the eraser of his pencil at my leg.

"Excellent," I said. "Just excellent. Pretty soon I'll be able to ice skate again."

I got into my car and sat behind the wheel. The young man remained at my side. He leaned on the window of my car and kept talking. "Boy, 235!" he said. "Splendid time, really."

I thanked him again and shook his hand before I drove off.

I was feeling wonderful—free and light-hearted. Even after the Nuerburgring in 1931 I hadn't felt like this. So things were working out—I was still able to drive. Indeed, I felt I could have got a lot more out of that car. There was only one dark cloud on my bright horizon. Would I be able to last when the speed got above 80 or 100 kilometers, when I had to sit behind the wheel for three or four hours? It was my luck that Mercedes was not participating in this year's Avus race, so I could spare myself a while without drawing attention.

But then, at the Grand Prix of Germany, I entered my name for the first time. I drove the hard and difficult course of the Nuerburgring and fought bitterly for first place with Stuck. When I had gained it, my motor conked out and I had to drop out. I had driven only half the race and again the question remained whether I could last 500 kilometers.

In August I entered the Klausen Pass mountain race. The course was only 22 kilometers long and of the other contenders I had only one to fear: Hans Stuck of Auto-Union.

But I was obsessed with another thought: In 1932 I had broken the record for that course and it hadn't been broken since. How would it be if I broke my own record now? Then I could prove that I had regained my old form—that I had, in fact, surpassed it.

The days of training were rainy and dismal. The tops of the mountains disappeared in the clouds and from there broad stretches of fog steamed down into the valley. The road itself glistened wetly. The motorcycles and sports cars started ahead of us. Everyone drove carefully. And the speed was way below the average of previous years.

When the race took place, on Sunday, a bright sun was in the sky. It was an unusual race. I was aware that I had to give it everything—and so I drove, from the very first, at top speed. I never saw my competitors, but only heard the roar of my own motor and drove for many minutes entirely alone. When I arrived at the summit I had broken my own record. I had driven the fastest time of the entire day, twenty seconds faster than three years before. I had proved that I was still the man I had been—on that short course.

14

In the fall I entered my name for the Grand Prix of Italy, in Monza. The race was to take place in September. It was the last Grand Prix of the year and the race went over 500 kilometers. We arrived in Milan at the end of August. Brauchitsch and Fagioli were the two other Mercedes drivers. Auto-Union was represented by Stuck, Momberger and Prince Leiningen; and Alfa had Varzi, Count Trossi and Chiron. Maserati was sending Nuvolari on the course.

It was a murderously hot autumn and we practiced on the course every day. The Italians had rebuilt the course since the previous year. They had devised an intricate system of various twists, such as hairpin curves and soft-shouldered bends. You had to shift and brake continually, hardly ever taking your hand off the gearshift. "A real mountain race without mountains," said Bubi Momberger. Even so, some pretty good speed was clocked.

The Alfa people got up to 2.25 to 2.28 minutes per lap. I managed 2.24 but Stuck outdid us all. He did a lap in 2.16.

The evening before the race we sat together in a bar in Milan. Neubauer was discussing our chances. He always did that with loving thoroughness but I could not bear to listen any longer and got up and went outside. I had enough trouble with my own worries. What good were his tactical tricks if my leg didn't come through?

The night was humid, the sky was overcast. A feeling of rain was in the air. Not a star in sight. I drove up the road to the Piazza del Duomo. Many people were up and about; the crowd was moving noisily through the street. The night was so hot and sticky the entire city was a vast steam bath. There was the cathedral, white in the bright beam of floodlights, its spire lost in the dark night sky. From the taverns came light and the babble of many voices and in front of the open doorways the people sat on the sidewalks.

I had made a dinner date in one of the restaurants with some other drivers. In spite of the rivalry we had a binding friendship among ourselves and we liked being together. We usually avoided talking about our cars—just as everyone avoids asking intimate questions. Usually the talk was about past races. That night Brivio told about his experiences in Sweden, of his superstitions which, incidentally, are widespread in Italy. On one occasion he had arrived too late to practice properly and he was less than enthusiastic about the course. That morning, a sparrow had flown through his window and alighted on his breakfast table. His mood shot down to zero. Birds, it was said, only come into the rooms of the dead. Nevertheless, he won the race that day.

In his lazy, elegant way our friend Trossi withstood questions about his clattery, brand-new, capricious, privately designed automobile. We all suggested he continue practicing into the night so he'd have time enough during the day to start his motor. Everyone talked about his own experiences, and, since most of us had driven at the same time, often about experiences during the same race. And everyone regarded a race from his own point of view, which made the experience different for each.

One had entered the race with an inferior car; the other with failing brakes; yet another with a hard steering mechanism. But they all had one goal before their eyes—not to give up, and, once in the lead, then there was only one aim: to win.

Only the drivers themselves knew what immense will power is needed in order to drive—in spite of smashed goggles, of painful blisters on the hands, of burning feet and of ribs chafed raw —a race to the finish. . . . And thus we sat, and the next day we would battle each other.

The year before on the eve of the Monza race, there had been more contestants. Chiron told how cheerful they had all been, how they had made Campari sing, how they had laughed about him and the way he forced his bulk down in his Alfa Monoposto. Before the race he had admired a chronometer, donated by Pirelli, and said that after the race which he intended to win he would like to have at least two of those. Also, he had told the mechanics to put aside a whole roast chicken for him because he would come back with a wolf's hunger. But he never came back from the first lap; nor did Borzacchini. Before the second race that day the drivers had been notified that there was an oil slick in the long curve, but that attempts had been made to clean the course. Sand had been spread over it. When the time for the third race came, late in the afternoon, the spot was apparently obliterated. Campari and Borzacchini careened off the course at full speed.

A deathly silence enveloped the stands and the course. What had happened seemed incredible. Even so, the last part of the race was to be held.

The rivals were Czaikowsky of Bugatti, and Lehoux. Everyone would have understood if both of these drivers had refused to start—that's how depressed the mood was in the racers' camp. Chiron told me that Lehoux had tried to make a deal with Czaikowsky not to open up to full speed until the last few laps. It hardly seemed right to challenge fate once more on this illomened day. But Czaikowsky refused to go along with the notion.

So he, too, failed to return after the last race. He had been thrown off the course at the same spot as Campari and Borzac-chini.

All three drivers were brought to lie in state. Green fir-tree branches decked the walls and you could not see the coffins for flowers and wreaths. Their friends passed by in silence, and the public crowded in awe before the dead heroes of the racing sport.

But we drivers kept our colleagues fresh in our memories—their words, their actions, their personalities were always kept alive in our talks.

We had especially liked shy, boyish little Borzacchini. He had never had much money and when, after the Tripoli race, he had made quite a bit, his friends never stopped teasing him. That evening in the restaurant Chiron told us that he had seen little Borzacchini just before the fatal race coming across the pit yard with a heavy brief case. In his amusing way Chiron told us:

"I went to him and said, 'My God, that brief case looks heavy! I suppose you're carrying your millions in it.' Borzac-chini winked and said, 'Of course. I never let it out of my hands.' I said, 'But what are you doing with all that money?' 'You know,' Borzacchini whispered to me, 'I lock myself into my room at home, close the shutters, make sure that no one else is around, and then I count the bills. When I'm sure that they're all there, I turn on the fan and dance among the fluttering, floating thousand-lire bills.'"

This was one of the many stories told that night. The death of our comrades was not gruesome to us—to us it seemed as if they would reappear in the door any moment to join the conversation. Varzi had reached his tenth espresso. His friends had emptied the sixth magnum of champagne. Chiron's black eyes were growing smaller and smaller—and I was yawning. It was time to go home. The race would start late and we could sleep it off.

"*Cameriere, conto!*"

Outside, the moon shone through a rift in the clouds right

down on the cathedral. The cathedral looked like a fantastic moon structure. I made straight for the hotel and went to bed. But I could not fall asleep. The room was hot and sticky and the heat poured through each aperture of the lowered blinds.

What if I was thrown out at the curve tomorrow? "Another victim of the Monza course," the newspapers would say, and I couldn't help thinking how many had been left on the road. But it must be a good death, I thought; it must be a quick one. At least it would be better to go this way than to die in some lingering fashion. Then I was back on the aching point: Would I make it tomorrow? Would the leg last the whole race?

In front of my window the streetcar took a corner. All night long I heard the screeching brakes and the slamming of the guide against the overhead wires. I did not fall asleep till early morning.

The next day I drove into Monza. It was even hotter than the previous day. The wind had swept away the clouds during the night and the sun in the cloudless sky beat down relentlessly.

We were already there at eleven. Lots had been drawn for the starting line-up the previous day. I had got a good place, right in the front row. Next to me were Varzi and Brivio, behind them Nuvolari and Stuck. In all, there were fifteen cars and, according to the experts, the outcome of the race was wide open to speculation. As I did not want to tire my leg by standing around too long, I got into my car right away.

We were posted right in front of the stands and from where I sat I had a good view of the crowd. The benches were packed solid, people sitting close together. From here they looked like a field of wheat ruffled by the wind.

The military band droned while the engines muttered along with the music. Then the mechanics started the cars and jumped back. General Baistrocchi stepped forward, the signal flag in his hand. He lifted it—it fluttered briskly in the wind. Down came the flag.

Rudolf Caracciola at fourteen, in the garden of his home on the Rhine.

Rudolf Caracciola in a Fafnir, at the Stadion Race in 1922.

The 4-cylinder, 6-h.p. Ego, in which Caracciola won the Stadion race near Berlin in 1923.

Caracciola at twenty-two, at the Kraehberg Hill Climb, in a supercharged 1½-liter 4-cylinder Targa-Florio Mercedes.

Caracciola with his riding mechanic, Eugen Salzer, after winning the German Grand Prix (1926) in a supercharged straight-eight 2-liter Monza Mercedes.

Rudolf Caracciola with his first wife, Charlotte, who died in an avalanche while skiing at Arusa in 1934.

Rudolf Caracciola with his riding mechanic, Sebastian, before the Mille Miglia in Italy in 1931, which was to be one of his greatest victories. Charlotte Caracciola, at far right, is wishing him luck.

Caracciola with his riding mechanic on the Raticosa Pass during the 1931 Mille Miglia. Note the quality of the road surfaces of those days.

A Mercedes-Benz streamlined SSK racing car, built for the fast Avus Race in 1932.

The famous Alfa-Romeo Racing Team of 1932: Rudi Caracciola, Tazio Nuvolari, Mario Borzacchini and Giuseppe Campari.

Caracciola in the sleek 1932 P 3 Alfa-Romeo before the start of the Monza Grand Prix.

Caracciola with racing manager, Alfred Neubauer.

Setting records on the Avus Speed Track in Berlin, 1934.

Bernd Rosemeyer, the successful star of the Auto-Union Racing Team in the years 1936-37.

Kautz, Brauchitsch, and Caracciola at the pits in Bern, 1936.

The Mercedes-Benz Record car: 3-liter, 12-cylinder, supercharged motor, in a Grand Prix Chassis 1938, with special body.

Caracciola and Lang leading the race at the Avus Track (1937).

One minute to go at Pescara, Italy (1937).

Caracciola in one of the famed formula Mercedes racing cars, 6-liter W. 125 with supercharger.

The cars roared away. Two white cars shot past me, then a red one. The curves were so narrow that one had to slow down to 50 kilometers. When I passed the boxes the second time they held out a sign:

STU—FAG—VAR—CAR

So Stuck was in the lead, but Fagioli was right behind him. At least one from our stable, I was thinking. Shift, foot off the gas, brace, shift again. This course was murderous. I had figured that in the course of 500 kilometers one had to shift gears 2,500 times. The red car ahead of me came closer. Varzi! terrific, the courage with which that fellow sped around corners!

The sound of the wind whistling past the windshield grew shrill.

The sixth lap.

It came as a blow: Fagioli was pulling up at the pit and came to a stop. Did that mean he was going to drop out? If he did I was the only Mercedes man left in the race.

Seventh lap. In the curve before the stands I overtook Varzi. Now there was only Stuck ahead of me. The speed increased. I had to get that man in front of me!

Tenth lap. The pit signaled:

STU

CAR—20 sec.

LEI—6 sec.

The heat was intolerable. The sweat streamed down my forehead, scalding my eyes. The leg was beginning to hurt—a faint, grinding pain, still bearable. But what if it got worse?

I drove and drove and drove. . . .

Each time I passed the pits Neubauer raised the flag. That meant: faster, faster! Fagioli had indeed dropped out. His car was still standing at the pits—I could glimpse it as I raced past.

Twentieth lap. The sign:

STU

CAR—13 sec.

So I'd gained seven seconds. But Neubauer was still gesturing, waving both arms in the air: faster, faster, faster. . . .

Twenty-fifth lap. . . .

The pain in my leg got worse. I tried to ignore it. I saw the speedometer trembling toward 6000 rpm. and the man ahead of me whom I must overtake.

Thirtieth lap. The sign said ten seconds behind Stuck. There—a stab of pain. While shifting I had hit my elbow against the frame of the car. It hurt damnably and I had the feeling that the arm was swelling, getting thicker and thicker.

Thirty-fifth lap—the pits showed Stuck eighteen seconds ahead of me.

Fortieth lap. . . . Stuck first, Caracciola second—with thirty-five seconds distance between us. It was hopeless, I'd never get that man. My body was numb, a steaming mass. I felt only the arm, and the leg. Oh yes, that leg—each time I applied the brake I felt a knife going through my thigh. Should I give up, pull up at the pits?

No!

If I gave up this race I'd give myself up. So—give her gas and put on speed.

Fiftieth lap. . . .

STU

CAR—20 sec.

Twenty seconds! Thank God, twenty again. So I'd gained some, in spite of everything. Faster, faster—Neubauer raised his flag again to give the signals.

Fifty-fifth lap—distance between Stuck and Caracciola, 18 seconds. A hellish race!

The pain in my leg was so bad I thought I would collapse any second now. It wouldn't matter. It wouldn't be bad, just as long as this ended.

Fifty-six, fifty-seven, fifty-eight laps. . . .

Only twelve seconds distance now. Now I could see him.

His white car appeared ahead of me and disappeared again in the next bend.

Fifty-ninth lap: Stuck pulled up at the pit, stopped for gas and tire change.

Now to leap ahead—and put on the final burst. I couldn't go on; it was asking more than was humanly possible. It felt as if my leg was being sawed off while I was fully conscious. . . .

And what now?

Admit that you are an invalid, that you can't last through a race any more?

No!

Never!

Once more I slammed my elbow full force against the steel plate of the car. It hardly hurt; the hellish firebrand in my leg numbed all other sensations.

Sixtieth lap. I raced up to the pits and stopped. The mechanics came running.

"Fagioli, get Fagioli to relieve me!" I shouted. "Quick, we've got to hold first place."

They started changing tires but I shook my head.

"Don't—the tires will last," I croaked. My throat was parched dry.

Fagioli jumped into the car. The motor howled and Fagioli was off and running. My car was still first; Stuck hadn't passed it yet.

I went back, into the back of the pit, walking very straight and trying not to let my leg drag. Back there it was cool and silent. I was all alone. The others were standing out front, eyes on the course.

I sat down on a canister and stretched out my miserable leg. Outside, the cars were roaring past, Fagioli still in the lead.

"What's the matter with you? Anything wrong?"

Dr. Glaeser, the track physician, was standing in front of me. I couldn't talk, merely pointed to my right arm in silence.

Gently Dr. Glaeser pulled down the sleeve—the elbow was suffused with blood, black and blue, and terribly swollen.

Dr. Glaeser bandaged my arm. I was indifferent to what was being done to my body. There was only one thought in my head, more painful than anything else: You didn't make it, you didn't last. . . .

From outside came a roar of applause, Neubauer's trumpet voice audible above all else.

"Bravo, Luigi, bravo!"

Fagioli had won. He was an Italian and it was a popular victory. The people were cheering wildly as we went up to the stand to receive our trophy.

15

I did not want to go back into the mountains that winter. The memory of it all was still too fresh. So I decided to take a trip to the States. I wanted to see what the racing business was like over there. The American drivers had a fabulous reputation. Fantastic speeds were being talked of. But—oddly enough—none of those who came from over there had been able to make out on European courses.

On the pier in New York, a representative of the Automobile Club, and George Robertson, a former champion, awaited me. They had heard I was coming and insisted on meeting me on my arrival.

"How are you?" said Mr. Robertson. "Did you have a good trip?"

He was an interesting sort. A slender sportsman with hard, sharply cut features. He told me at once that they were going to build a race course outside the city.

"A course in the shape of a pretzel, you understand," he said. "You can watch the entire race from every place in the stands."

We went to my hotel and from there to a very fine club. Here Robertson explained to me the difference between American and European automobile racing.

"Over there you build road racers," he said, "with five or six gears. We build our cars exclusively for the race course.

They have only two gears and if they race off the curves we change the course, but not the cars. The art of driving? Well, yes. But the people here want speed. That's what they come to see."

In the evening I was Robertson's guest. He lived in a magnificent apartment house on Fifth Avenue. When I drove up light misty rain was falling. A canopy covered the sidewalk from the door to the curb, with a red carpet on the ground beneath it. A doorman with gold-braid on his uniform opened the car and led me to the elevator, which shot upward quickly and soundlessly. A click—we stopped at the thirty-second floor. I got out and found myself right in the middle of Robertson's living room. He came over to me, greeted me warmly: "Hello, old boy!"

I was introduced to the other guests. At first I thought they were trying to pull my leg, but then I realized that they were being quite genuine. All asked exactly the same questions, just as if they had agreed on them beforehand.

"How was the trip over? How long will you stay here? Please be sure and come to see us." Then a handshake and on to the next one where the whole thing was repeated.

The women looked almost all alike. Most of them were blond, long-legged and conventionally good looking. There was a lot of drinking, and toward midnight the party was in a gay mood. They kept laughing about things I could not, much as I tried, find in the least bit funny.

Right after midnight I went to Robertson and said goodby. I told him I was going to start out early the next morning on a cross-country trip and had to get up at dawn. He wasn't in the least offended. He gave me a recommendation to Pop Meyers because I had told him that I wanted to see the speedway in Indianapolis, and then he advised me by all means to see a midget race.

"You don't have anything like it in Europe," he said.

He went down the elevator with me, shook my hand, and I had to promise to visit him again on my return to New York.

The next morning at daybreak, I got in my Mercedes and took off. When I got out of the city I took a deep breath of relief. It was a fresh January morning, the air was clear and bright as glass and a pale blue sky arched over the landscape. It was a completely flat vista. You could see how, on the horizon, sky and earth came together, and when the road led straight ahead it gave you the feeling of driving straight into the sky.

Those roads were wonderful, broad and straight and lined with trees. Since it was still early morning and not many other vehicles were on the road—only a few trucks, loaded with produce, clattered past me on their way to New York.

A little way beyond Middletown I observed, in the rear-view mirror, a small Ford trailing me. Obviously he wanted to pass me. I don't like being passed; an occupational characteristic, I suppose. So I stepped on the gas and took off with a roar. The speedometer showed 100, then 120 kilometers (75 mph.) but the Ford stayed right behind me, in fact it seemed as if the distance between us had shrunk.

I went up to 150. Then there was a railroad crossing and I had to slow down. The Ford was catching up quickly. In the mirror I saw it crossing the tracks without slowing down. Oh well, I thought, if that's the way you want it. I slowed down. There was no point in fighting an opponent as unfair as that. The Ford pulled up swiftly. There were two state troopers in it. When they had reached me, one of them waved at me to stop. I stopped and so did they.

Then one of them got out and came over to my car. He was a fresh-faced fellow with a nice boyish smile under a wide-brimmed hat. On his belt he wore a revolver that slammed against his hip with every step. He saluted and, smiling, asked for my driver's license.

I showed it to him. He thanked me, handed it back to me and then asked me, still smiling, to turn around and drive alongside them to Easton. I wanted to ask him why, but he was already back in his car. So, side by side, we drove back.

At the entrance to Easton there was a small red-brick house. There we stopped. I got out and the young man with the wide hat opened the door for me. We entered a rather bare room with a table and a chair in the middle, where sat an older man with a burgundy-red face and snow-white hair. When we came in he took his feet off the table, closed a lurid-covered detective novel and regarded me with calm gray eyes.

The two state troopers saluted and one of them said:

"Speeding, Lieutenant."

"How fast?"

"About eighty, sir."

He turned to me.

"Is that true?"

"Yes."

"Twenty dollars," he said.

"I'm a foreigner and I don't know how fast I'm allowed to drive here," I said.

"The legal speed limit is forty-five miles," he informed me. "Do you want to pay or do you want a hearing in court?"

I looked at him. He seemed to be a quiet, friendly man and I didn't think I could get away cheaper elsewhere.

"I'll pay," I decided.

"Right," he said.

I took two ten-dollar bills from my wallet and put them on the table. He opened a drawer and swept the bills into it.

"Thank you," he said and reached for his detective novel. With that he dismissed me.

The troopers escorted me to the door. One of them obliged

me by showing me the shortest route to the next town. When I took off they both stood there saluting me, hands raised to their wide-brimmed hats.

Actually I had wanted to watch a midget race in Chicago, but when I stopped over in Middletown I found that they were having a race there just then. I was sitting in a restaurant and happened to see the poster on the wall. It was a very impressive poster—out of a cloud of dust a racing car drove straight at the observer. I inquired about it and learned that the race track was just outside the town. It was half past three. The race had started at three. Off I went.

You could see the track from quite a way off. A vast number of cars was parked outside—at least four thousand, according to my estimate.

To be a midget racer is a neck-breaking profession. Many reckless young men have lost their lives in that wild sport, but if a year goes by without an accident, their income is considerable.

I studied the little cars closely. Those short, narrow one-seaters were worked out exquisitely, down to the smallest detail. Every car that went to the start was a little gem. Chassis and frame were built superlight, all hand-made, and they saved on weight where they could.

Except for the motor everything had to be very light and cheap because—who knows?—perhaps the whole caboodle would meet its destiny in the first curve.

In front, in back, even on the sides there were rounded bumpers so that the cars wouldn't get hooked to one another. The drivers lashed themselves to the seats to avoid being thrown out on the road if they collided or turned upside down, in which case the cars following would inevitably pile up over them. Crash helmets were obligatory.

The contrast between the tiny cars and the athletic figures who drove them was, of course, almost grotesque. The drivers stuck way out of their vehicles and I wondered how they ever managed to squeeze into their seats. Many of them wore high leather boots to protect their legs in case of fire.

The start was like that on a horse-race track—as soon as the pack of cars were properly placed the starter lowered the flag and climbed to a high seat from where he could survey the race. The start was breath-taking, a wild confusion. No more than inches apart the cars skidded through the curves. After a few laps the field gradually drew apart, the known drivers slowly pulled ahead, encouraged by the shouts of the spectators. I, too, infected by the excitement, found myself shouting:

"Come one! Step on it! Come on. . . ."

It didn't seem in the least odd that my neighbor keeping time with the shouts, was beating the man in front of him on the head with a newspaper—and the victim wasn't even conscious of it.

But the mood was not only one of enthusiasm. There was something else in the air, something ominous, threatening. Everyone seemed to be apprehensive of something.

Attention began to focus on two cars—a black one and a red one. The red one was very close to the black one—so very close, and yet it made no attempt to overtake it. It was the red one that had the spectators' sympathy.

Next to me there was a group of young fellows—apprentice drivers, I gathered. Their faces were stiff with tension as they stared into the roaring maelstrom below, like hawks awaiting their prey.

"What's the matter with those two down there?" I asked them, pointing to the two cars.

A youngster turned to me and the others also glanced around.

"He's going to get even with him today," the youngster said, and they all grinned.

Desperately the black car tried to detach itself from its pursuer, but the red one followed him closely, like a shadow.

"What's he want to get even about?" I asked, offering him a cigarette. He took it and said, without looking at me:

"Because Bob—that's the black one—cut him off once. Joe, the red one, broke his leg that time. Today he's going to get even for that. We've waited a long time for this day."

While he was talking we all looked down at the track. It had become strangely quiet all around. The red pursuer was sneaking up from the side now. The yellow warning light flashed up at the starter's stand. But at that instant it happened. The two cars collided, turned over and lay with their wheels spinning in the air. Flame arose. Fire engines roared up to the scene of the accident. The other cars were being kept back.

With much effort the red driver was dragged out of his car—his leg was still in plaster and, as luck would have it, only the plaster was singed. The black driver seemed to have been injured more severely. Ambulance men carried him on a stretcher into the gray tent. An attendant dragged the wreckage from the track through the main exit.

All this happened terribly fast, much faster than I can tell it. Again cars drove up to the start and the orange-colored helper was running back and forth, grabbing one, then the other, pushing them off. The cars rattled away, humming around the track.

Slowly I left the stand. I was still numb. They were incredible fellows, those midget drivers, fearless and daring, and they could drive. Like most of us they seemed to think: it won't hit me!

I found my car, got in and drove off. I traveled up the highway in the direction of Pittsburgh. I heard the sound of the race for a long time as I sped along the road. From afar it was like a swarm of bees humming in the hive.

16

When I arrived in Indianapolis I went to the hotel right away. The next day I called Pop Meyers. When he heard that I wanted to see the race track, he said he would pick me up in half an hour.

I went to my room and changed, and when I came down there he was—with American punctuality—sitting in the hotel lobby. I knew him from innumerable pictures I had seen of Indianapolis races—smooth-shaven, full-faced, with white hair and kindly blue eyes behind rimless glasses.

We said hello and had a few drinks together, talking about the European races. Then we drove out together in his Packard.

The course is about ten miles outside of town. On the way it began to rain, and when we arrived the wind was blowing a chilling squall across the course. It was a most depressing sight: the wide oval with the rows of empty benches, the brickwork of track below reflecting the rain, and in the background a few bare trees bending to the storm. It had the quality of a vast ruin, like a deserted Roman arena.

"You should see this when the race starts," said Pop Meyers with a sweeping gesture of his hand. "A hundred and seventy thousand spectators. They sit everywhere, up in the trees, even; and the youngsters climb up the flagpoles. And then that big gate over there opens and the military band comes marching in. Last year we had six bands. They march around the whole track and then they post themselves before the main grandstand. All the people get to their feet—and then a great silence falls over the crowd. Three minutes' silence. Those are three minutes of commemoration of the dead who gave their lives to the sport."

Down below, along the track, wooden shacks were standing in the rain—garages, pit, little tool sheds.

"You should see," Pop Meyers said, pointing to where the shacks stood like leftovers from a country fair, "three weeks before the race, what they look like. That's when the boys are down there in the shacks tinkering with their machines day and night. Most of them drive the same make, but each has contributed some special, private invention of his own on which he puts all his hopes. Twenty thousand dollars, Mr. Caracciola, is a lot of money for any one of those guys. And they keep hoping and working for weeks before the races, every year. There are some among them who've been waiting for their chance for years.

"And then the training for the race, Mr. Caracciola! You should be here when the regulations committee has them drive the qualification rounds, and those young fellows stand alongside the track, waiting. As soon as a driver drops out for any reason, they rush to take his place. The manager of an outfit has only to snap his fingers and there are ten, twenty boys ready to take over—boys who don't care a damn for their own lives and take off as if they were possessed. It's happened more than once that one of those youngsters that no one had ever heard of before, got behind the wheel and drove himself home a prize. Give them all a break, that's our motto."

I was amazed. What a marvelous country, what a marvelous setup! I recalled how hard it had been for me to break into the game. What a long, hard painful road it had been until they let me take the wheel of a racing car for the first time.

And here, a young fellow had only to show up, and with some luck he might even make it!

The rain became heavier. We got into the car and went back to town. On the way Pop Meyers told me a lot more about his race track, and I thought of the days when I started with Alfa and of the hard times the old guard of the Alfa team had given me.

17

It had never occurred to me to give up my profession. But this time, I knew, if I failed another race—if my leg didn't come through—then I had no choice; I would have to leave the track forever.

The next race took place in Tripolis, in the spring of 1935. We were to embark at Naples, and I drove down in my car, alone. Going through Brescia I remembered the Mille Miglia. Once I had succeeded in mastering this—for foreigners—almost invincible course. I had driven my white SSK Mercedes to victory and had driven joyfully into Brescia.

And I had been there again, three years ago, when I started working for Alfa. I remembered it so vividly . . . the car breaking down in Verona and the mechanic and I trotting through the strange town in the early light of dawn and looking for the Alfa representative. Finally we located him and knocked at the door of his apartment till he woke up. He appeared in the doorway barefooted, clad in a long white nightshirt. Then, when he recognized us, he became eager and helpful, pulled on a pair of pants and got hold of a Fiat for us in which we drove over to Brescia, the last station of the course. When we arrived there the sun was just coming up. The stands were empty and in the cold early morning they looked awfully deserted. The last cars had arrived the previous evening and no one had expected us any more. We were about to drive on but suddenly a small female figure in a gray coat got up. She had crouched there all night long, in the front row. Now she arose and came down the stands toward me.

It was Charly. She put her arms around my neck and pressed her face against mine. She was trembling all over and her face was ice cold, and I felt my cheeks grow wet with her tears. Charly had found it was hard to be a racing driver's wife. . . .

Well—that was over, all over now. . . . Now I was driving from Bologna via Florence and Rome down to Naples, and from there we were to ship over to Tripolis where the next race was taking place. It was very important for me to win this race—in fact, it was vital.

Everywhere, in all the cities I was passing through, there were enormous posters announcing the "Lotteria di Tripoli," the big lottery of 36 millions that was tied up in the race. At all the street corners stood invalids—old men, women and cripples—selling tickets for twelve lire apiece; everybody in Italy had a stake in that race.

In Naples I met the others—Brauchitsch, Fagioli and Neubauer. They had arrived half a day earlier and now they sat in the bar of the hotel drinking *apéritifs*. When I came in they greeted me noisily—we hadn't seen each other since Monza and I had been in the States in the meantime. We had dinner in the hotel and went aboard early. By ten P.M. we were moving out of the harbor.

It was a rainy night. No stars could be seen, only the lights in the harbor; and above, in the black sky the breath of Vesuvius glowed.

It seemed as if the ship had been chartered solely for the race drivers. Auto-Union was aboard and the people from Scuderia Ferrari who were driving Alfa. We all met on the upper deck in the bar and drank and swapped memories.

Neubauer put on swimming trunks, and in the guise of Neptune, delivered a speech. The Italians drank chianti as if they were being paid for it and everyone grew louder and funnier the later it became. I tried to keep up with them for quite a while, but then I got up and went out on deck.

The night wind blew and a spume rose up from the bow. The sea was absolutely black. I went to the upper deck of the second-class section where our cars had been stashed away. They stood under gray tarpaulins, with a ship's lantern shining down on them from a mast. They looked almost like a herd of great, sleeping sheep.

Next to our cars stood those of Auto-Union and Alfa. I made my way among the cars and looked at everything. From a bench a man got up and wandered over to my side. He was a mechanic from Alfa who was standing watch. I knew him slightly from Milan.

"Good evening, Mr. Caracciola. *Tutto bene?*"

"Yes, thank you."

We stepped up to the rail together.

"How's your two-engine Alfa?" I asked.

"The engines are fine," he said. "But they'll use up the tires fast with that weight, I'm sure."

I offered him a cigarette and lit one myself. We stood side by side staring down into the dark water that flowed swiftly by. Then I went back down to the afterdeck.

There was a coil of rope—I sat down on it and looked out across the dark sea. Two dim ribbons of foam trailed behind the ship. You could see them for a while, then they were gone, gobbled up by the darkness of this endless night. Loud voices were coming from the bar—I could not understand the words, but everyone still seemed very cheerful up there. Would they all return from Tripolis? Or would someone be torn from our ranks again?

How few remained of those who had started out with me, twelve years earlier! Stuck was still there, and Brauchitsch, Varzi, Nuvolari, Chiron. The others, the ones who had come later, were kids—a new generation. A career behind the steering wheel soon devours a man's life. It is as if the racing heart of the motor were forcing our lives into a faster tempo, too, as if our blood and our nerves were used up faster.

Dead—crashed—retired. . . . Retired, and what then? Become a private citizen? Raise flowers somewhere in a peaceful corner of the world or start a business venture? Hard to imagine —in fact, unthinkable. But what else?

There was only one way of life for us—to call up our last reserve of power and fight to the finish.

But suppose my body failed me—the leg gave out, this time and over and over again? Or if one just grew older and couldn't keep pace because the youngsters were pushing one aside? If one was simply used up, finished, burned out?

Then what?

Dawn began to break. A gray morning. I shivered and went down to my cabin.

I did not appear on deck until eleven. The clouds had vanished. It was a bright, sunny morning. Our people were topside, lolling in deck chairs, Neubauer among them. He had his hat over his face, his belly high in the air. He was expounding racing strategy. From under his hat he kept talking in Fagioli's direction because he considered him the victor in the coming race.

The next morning land came into sight and shortly afterward we saw Tripolis. The wind had turned southward and brought a dry, sultry heat that seemed to press down upon the lungs and drew sweat from every pore.

"That's the *ghibli*," said Fagioli who was leaning over the rail nearby. "God help us if we have the *ghibli* Sunday, during the race."

The sky was yellowish gray, and from that yellow-gray sky the city stood out ghostly white. As we came nearer I noticed that the air was filled with dust, a fine reddish dust that brought tears to the eyes and gritted in one's teeth with every word.

"That's the taste of Africa," said Fagioli, laughing.

In the harbor stood single, horse-drawn carriages, one after the other. We each chartered one and rode down the street toward our hotel. It was a splendid avenue skirting the shore—white houses and cupolas on one side, the sea on the other. The street itself was lined with tall palms whose fronds clattered in the wind. But the *ghibli* cast a yellow veil of dust over the entire scene, extinguishing all colors.

The hotel was magnificent—cedarwood and marble, a show place built by the Italian government. I went up to my room almost immediately but I couldn't close my eyes all night. The dreadful heat lay on my chest like a sack of damp, hot wash. Several times when I turned on the light I saw little clouds of red dust drifting across the parquet floor.

Practice began the next morning. The track was outside the town, amid the salt flats. A snow-white, tall tower stood at the starting line, towering above the great mass of the stone stands like a church spire.

The first day, all participants appeared at the start. The *ghibli* was still blowing from the south, though not as strong as it had been the previous day. But the fine red dust was still there.

The Alfa people started first. Then when their small, red cars had vanished roaring into the dust veil of the desert sand, it was our turn. First Fagioli, then I, then Brauchitsch. Fagioli took the lead as pacemaker, increasing the speed from lap to lap. Behind me, in the rear-view mirror, I saw Brauchitsch. In the sixth lap Brauchitsch stopped, and in the eighth I saw Fagioli pulling up to the pit. I really opened up then. During the tenth lap a shock went through the car; the rubber casing of a rear wheel had torn off and the tread hung down in shreds. I had to pull up at the pit.

"How fast did I go?" I asked, taking off my goggles.

"Three forty-five—the fastest lap," said a mechanic.

I glanced over at Neubauer.

"What's the use!" he thundered. "Suppose the tires are all blown to bits?"

Dietrich, the tire specialist from Continental, was standing right there. His face, with the upturned mustache, wore a worried frown.

"It's this heat," he said, "that eats up the tires."

Next to us, the cars of Auto-Union were being started. Their roar drowned all conversation. And now they were off, Varzi first and Stuck right behind him.

Neubauer timed the start with his stop watch. He stood there peering down the track oblivious of us all. I went around my car and contemplated the blown rear tire. It looked pretty bad. The rubber casing had loosened, and the naked lining was exposed.

Dietrich stepped up to me.

"If this happens to you, of all people, Mr. Caracciola, how bad is it going to be for the others?"

From far away a hum grew into a roar—there they were, Varzi first, then Stuck.

"Three fifty-two—from a standing start," said Neubauer.

Varzi and Stuck took one lap after the other. They seemed to be running a private race between themselves. They were now in the middle of the twelfth lap and still apparently no wear on their tires.

There was a heavy silence in our pit. We had all gone inside to find shelter from the heat and the *ghibli*. Only Neubauer had remained outside, standing in the burning sun and tirelessly clocking the speed of the Auto-Union drivers. He had pushed his hat on the back of his head and two big sweat stains were visible on the back of his gray shirt. Now he turned around and came toward the pit where we sat. You could tell from his face how excited he was.

"Varzi's best lap, 3.36; Stuck's 3.34!" He spoke out of the corner of his mouth toward the bench where we drivers sat. At that instant Stuck came thundering by outside and the entire pit was filled with the roar of his motor. "Three thirty-three!" Neubauer shouted over his shoulder. Even in his excitement he hadn't forgotten to clock the speed.

Then practice was called off and we went back to our hotel.

In the afternoon we all met in the hotel lobby. It was quiet and cool inside. The shades were down; somewhere in the background could be heard the gentle splashing sound of a fountain. Outside, the *ghibli* still blew.

"We'll have to change tires three times," said Neubauer. He tapped with his pencil on the marble table top. "Three times, I said, Herr von Brauchitsch."

Brauchitsch nodded sleepily.

Neubauer began theorizing. "That means we lose at least one minute three times. Because even if we reach our record of thirty seconds for one tire change, you have to figure on one minute, what with stopping and everything else. Now listen to me, gentlemen. I am sure that Auto-Union is going to have only two tire changes. And after what I've seen during practice today, they can get away with two changes. You can easily figure what that means. One minute's advantage in any case. One minute that we're bound to lose at the pit."

He looked at us, each in turn. We were silent.

What he says makes sense, I thought. But there were so many unforeseeable possibilities . . . so much could happen in a race. For instance, my leg could go back on me . . . and there I was again with my painful problem.

Neubauer's head was bent over his notebook. He was scribbling figures.

"So then we must be at least one and a half seconds faster than our opponents on every lap if we want to have a chance at all," he said.

"Or else drive more slowly and save our tires," put in Brauchitsch, getting up and wandering in the direction of the bar. Neubauer made a disapproving sound and with that the lesson in theory ended.

In the evening we went slumming in the native quarter. We went through the narrow alleys and wound up in a café in which, so it was said, a naked Arab girl was supposed to be dancing. The place was hot and smoky and crowded with Italian colonial soldiers. The girl was not Arab and didn't dance well. Besides, she wasn't naked.

We drank Turkish coffee while Neubauer again began calculating the rpm's we could expect from the cars without damaging them. It wasn't a particularly amusing evening.

I finally said good-by to the others and went alone to where my car was parked. I got in and drove along the shore road, out into the countryside.

The moon was shining but the *ghibli* had not let up, and I was moving through a cloud of dust. The moon shimmered through that dust, making an uncertain kind of light, a good deal like the foggy moonlights in the extreme north. I headed for the track and then drove around it once more—an entire lap, very slowly, reviewing once again all the observations I had made during practice. Once, I stopped in the middle of the track, got out, and removed a stone from the roadway. It might happen, after all, that the ground crew would overlook it next morning. I stood there awhile listening to the roar of the surf above the wind. The sea was just at hand.

I got back into the car and drove on. I was thoroughly calm now. The following day would decide everything, and any decision was preferable to the torturous uncertainty of the past months. It would be bad, of course, if the engine broke down or I got stranded on the course with a blown tire. Then I would have to wait again. And it was the waiting that was worst of all.

18

The million-lire race was scheduled for the following day. The *ghibli* was still with us. When we posted ourselves at the start, the sky was a sulfurous yellow.

We stood alongside our cars and waited. From the stands came the intermittent strains of music, interrupted by the sudden roar of an engine, and up on the veranda of the timekeeper's booth lots were being drawn. For a moment I tried to listen—I'd have liked to know who had drawn my lot. But down here I couldn't catch a word. The announcer's voice came through the loudspeaker like the barking of a dog.

We were waiting for Marshal Balbo, the governor. I was standing in the third row, next to Varzi. At last he arrived; an escort of twelve motorcycles raced ahead of him and then Balbo came into sight in his big, open car. The "Giovinezza" was struck up. The people on the stands arose and the soldiers who were standing on the lawn below the stands snapped to attention.

Balbo stopped directly next to the drivers and got out. He went through the rows, pausing before each driver and saying a few words. To me he spoke in German:

"Are you in good shape again?"

"Yes, your Excellency."

"Very good," he said, "*in bocca lupo!*" And he went on among us. He was a slim, medium-sized man with copper-

111

colored hair and beard, and he walked erect, with short quick steps. We climbed into our cars.

The large clock above the pits showed three minutes to three. One minute to three. Over his shoulder Marshal Balbo gave an order to one of the soldiers standing on the parapet behind him. The soldier jumped down and ran off.

The engines were started and the mechanics jumped aside.

The track was free. Balbo lifted the flag. I looked away from him and fixed my gaze on the signal light of the timekeeper's booth. Perhaps this technique is faster, I thought. And when the green light flashes on, I'm off. Otherwise I thought of nothing. Four—three—two. . . . The green light! I shifted, the car shot ahead, past the others. I was in the lead, ahead of everybody at the start.

At full speed I shot into the straightaway. Everything took place almost automatically, as it often did—every move had been rehearsed. I knew the course so well now that I could drive in my sleep.

Now the white tower, the stands, the pits were gone. And no sign from the pits. The first lap, the second—again the pits, and there, for the first time, the sign:

CAR
NUV
VAR

So the two Italians were behind me. It'd be a tough battle if they forced their speed up. I must go faster, much faster. . . . Fourth lap: CAR, VAR, NUV. So the man from Milan had overtaken the fellow from Mantua once again. Now he was right on my neck—a dangerous opponent. And in an Auto-Union car, at that!

Sixth lap—the white tower, the enormous structure of the stands. Then suddenly, the left front tire turned long and thin, something flew past me: the casing had torn itself loose. Foot off the gas, brake, over to the pits.

A white car shot past me—Varzi.

I took a gulp of water, slapped a wet towel on my hot forehead. . . . Two cars came thundering by—Stuck and Fagioli. A few last taps with the copper hammer on the front wheel and I was off. Twenty seconds lost—thank God, only twenty seconds! Stuck and Fagioli weren't far ahead yet. I was streaking straight into the cloud of dust they had left behind in the bend.

Eighth lap: VAR, CAR—13. So I had gained back seven of the twenty lost seconds. And Varzi would have to stop too, eventually.

Still the eighth lap—the long straightaway beside the shore. A shock went through the car—I couldn't see it, but I could feel it. The tread of a back tire was gone. I still had the car under control. Slow down! A white car pulled past me. Stuck or Fagioli—I couldn't tell which. Only now I began to notice how hot it was. My clothes stuck to my skin and my lips were cracked and dry.

Over to the pits! Neubauer shouted, throwing his arms into the air but I couldn't understand what he was saying. All four tires were being changed. The tank was being filled. This took one minute and ten seconds. In the meantime eight cars went shooting past—first, three singly, then an entire cluster. I'd fallen back to tenth place.

Everything inside me was in a tremor. One of the mechanics yelled into my ear:

"The tires will fly off the others too! Just wait!"

Neubauer, with a scowl on his face, stood looking at his stop watch.

One minute and ten seconds. Just as I drove off, a white car came blazing past me into the curve: Varzi in the Auto-Union. He had beaten me around the turn and was leading the field by an entire lap. I couldn't possibly catch up with him now. It was really quite hopeless, and if I kept on with the race it was only to maintain the honor of the firm.

I crept up close to Varzi, I passed him—but what was the use of it all? The heat was unbearable. My skull was roaring and my tongue hung dry in my mouth like a flap of leather. I was raging with thirst—and I no longer hoped for anything.

I hadn't expected this. I had really thought that fate would have a clear answer for me this time. And now I had to fall back because of the absurd accident of a blown tire. The leg seemed all right—in fact, it was in fine shape. Now and then it hurt a little in the hip socket, but not enough to bother me. The thirst was far worse.

I kept on driving. I no longer knew what position I held in the race; I was floating around somewhere in the field. The pits were silent—no sign from them any more. They'd given me up.

Twelfth lap. . . . Varzi roared up to the pits and stopped there. Probably tire trouble, too. Let the Auto-Union drivers see what it feels like to be pulled away from the lead! Racing past, I caught a glimpse of our sign: Fagioli was leading by thirty-six seconds. . . . Well, at least one of us was ahead.

Around the wide bend—there, in the agave underbrush, was a car with its wheels in the air. A hundred meters farther on, two ambulance men were carrying a stretcher. They were going along at a trot. Who was it? Dead—injured? Presently they were out of sight.

Sixteenth lap. . . . Again the dull shock. I knew the feeling by now without having to look. The back tire was shot. It was just before the long straightaway by the sea. There was the emergency depot—I pulled up. They had seen me coming far away and they literally jumped on the car. Now for that water —avidly, greedily, I poured the lukewarm water into me.

"Who was that back at the agaves?"

"Brivio."

"Dead?"

"No. . . ."

"Badly hurt?"

The mechanic shrugged—he didn't know.

Right behind me the cars thundered past once again. White, red—singly, in pairs close up, vying for position. At the depot they worked rapidly and in less than a minute I was on the track again.

One minute, which meant I was now almost four minutes' distance from the leading car. It was no use—but I had to go on. I shouldn't have drunk all that water. The sweat was pouring down my body now and my mouth was already as dry as before.

Eighteenth lap. . . . There was a busy crowd at the pits. Apparently many of the cars had been forced to stop. On and on. At kilometer marker no. 8, just alongside the track, a car had burst into flames. A white car—meaning a German.

Twentieth lap. A sign from the pit, the first one in a long while. Thank God!

VAR

FAG

DREY

CAR—2.36

So I was in fourth place now. I had regained a minute and twenty-four seconds in less than five laps. Very good! So there was hope yet. There was still a dim chance. But now this meant getting everything there was to get out of the car. I was going at such a speed that the little Alfas I passed seemed to be standing still—I must have climbed to 270 kilometers at least. During the twenty-fifth lap another sign from the pits: I was in second place—one minute and thirty-two seconds behind Varzi. So I had gained back another minute and four seconds in the past five laps.

Should I put on speed? No. Be calm, be clear, think straight, I told myself. I must go easy on the tires, I mustn't strain them the way I had in the beginning. If I got stuck with torn tires once more, I'd never have the time to catch up because the race ended with the fortieth lap. After the twenty-seventh lap I drove up to the pit to get all four tires changed for the last time. With this set I intended to last through to the finish.

Neubauer himself put a wet towel on my head. "Nice going, Rudi," he said. "Keep it up."

"Whose car's burning?"

"Stuck's."

The tires were changed in record time—in less than a minute I was off again. Nobody had overtaken me in the meantime and my distance from Varzi was one minute and forty-five seconds. With the new tires I increased my speed again—to the point where Neubauer was motioning me from the pits to slow down.

By the thirtieth lap my distance from Varzi had shrunk to forty-two seconds. Take it easy, I told myself; slow down. This time the tires have got to last! In the rear-view mirror I saw a red car creeping up, narrowing the distance. Nuvolari!

I thought rapidly, if I let him pass me, with his Alfa he wouldn't really be a threat. And the two who were ahead—those two old fighters, those furious, bitter rivals of so many great races—will battle each other, a battle in which Varzi, too, would exhaust his last reserves.

In the curve I let Nuvolari pass me and now the wild chase between the two of them was on. For two laps they raced side by side. Time after time the wiry little Mantuan tried to get Varzi and time after time he fell back.

Then Nuvolari dropped out. Tire trouble. He disappeared far back in the field. The pit held up a sign:

VAR

CAR

But the distance between us has widened to one minute.

Thirty-fifth lap. What if I had miscalculated? Was the man ahead of me driving on iron tires? Ah, he stopped at the emergency depot. But he was off again before I could catch him. However, the distance had shrunk to fourteen seconds.

Five more laps. I could see Varzi's car directly in front of me and I knew I had to get him, that I *would* get him. I poured on speed, regardless of consequences. The white Auto-Union car was less than a hundred meters ahead of me. Thirty-eighth lap. . . . I got him! In the bend I pulled past him. But the race wasn't over yet because he stuck behind me, so close that I could see him in the rear-view mirror all the time. I couldn't shake him off. He kept sitting right on my neck. When we passed the pits again the sign said:

CAR
VAR

But I knew that the man behind me was keeping the pace; his white car stuck tenaciously.

Thirty-ninth lap:

CAR
VAR

And again no distance was given—that's how close we were. Into the fortieth lap—the last. As we roared by the stands I saw the people jumping to their feet and gesticulating. The great bend behind the stands—the long shore-side straightaway. . . . And there, at last, the man behind me dropped back. The white car vanished from my mirror. The tower, now; the stands; the finish line . . . over!

But the momentum of the fierce spurt was too great—I had to let the car unwind for another lap before I brought it up to the pits.

For a moment I sat absolutely numb. The engine was silent. It was so strangely quiet around me. I pushed up my goggles and looked up at the stands. The people were sitting there almost motionless, staring out at the track. Only a few had jumped up and were waving at me. The rest were waiting for Varzi.

And then they were all around me—Neubauer and the mechanics, among them my faithful Walz. The big fellow was beside himself—he literally plucked me from the car, pressed me to him and kissed me on both cheeks. Two mechanics lifted me on their shoulders and carried me into the pit. I was shaking hands right and left but still I felt numb.

Then suddenly it dawned upon me: victory! Thank God, victory! It was a feeling impossible to describe, impossible to compare with anything. There was the sun, the people . . . everything was good and bright and friendly, and I was back— yes, that was the greatest marvel, I was back and I could fight again as well as all the rest. There would be happy days and sad ones, victories and defeats, strong competitors and weak ones. I would be angry or sad or happy, but the most beautiful thing of all would remain: the shadow was gone, I was back among the contenders.

Oh, and before I forget: The number that had been placed on my car had been picked by the head messenger in the Finance Ministry, a fellow named Gaetano Giacomini. He had paid only 10.50 lire for it instead of 12. With his wife and son, who was a hairdresser's apprentice, and with the rest of the family, he was at the radio all during the race. In his feverish excitement he promised his friends that if he won the big prize of six million lire he would distribute one million among them. Before the twentieth lap he started wailing that he had lost. Then when I won, he almost went out of his mind. He'd asked his boss for a leave, and fled town with his family. He wanted, perhaps out of superstition, to buy the car in which I'd won. So, by a fluke of fate, I had made the luck of a sixfold millionaire.

19

Contests and victories, successes and defeats! Old opponents vanished, new ones appeared. The pace was becoming faster and faster, the battle harder, more relentless as time went on. In 1935 luck was with me—with seven Grand Prix and two other races I had become German champion and had earned the European championship for Mercedes.

In 1936 young Bernd Rosemeyer won victory after victory and the European championship became his.

Nineteen thirty-seven was an important year for me. That year I won my greatest prize—a woman—a girl I had known for many years. She herself had been for some time part of the European racing society; all of us in the racing game liked and respected her for her steadfastness and helpfulness. Alice Hoffmann-Trobeck was known also for her remarkable ability with languages, and during races she was tops as a timekeeper. With a double chronometer she was unsurpassed, registering all cars, all speeds. She handled her clock as expertly as I did my steering wheel.

That time in Monte Carlo, when I had the dreadful accident during practice, she had been there. She had interpreted for me and Charly in our talks with the doctors at the hospital.

She had also come to Arosa with my sister Ilse when Charly was taken from me. And she was with me when I drove a racing car once more.

In the course of the next four years I saw her repeatedly at various races or in Paris or Berlin, and I began to feel more and more that she might be the ideal life partner for me. After my return from America I was certain of it; it simply had to be "Baby" Hoffmann-Trobeck and no one else.

Baby is a most positive little person and—well, optimistic. I've often asked myself where that small, frail creature gets all her energy and stamina.

"You know very well," she says. "Simply a mixture of Viking blood and Swedish steel."

She says it laughingly, but it's true. She has endured all the stress of our nomadic existence, and also uncomplainingly put up with the hard life I brought her with my accidents. She was forever hopeful, always ready to believe the sun would appear from behind the blackest cloud.

In June we were married in Lugano. My friends Dr. Wilhelm Haspel, later director general of the Daimler Benz AG; his wife, Bimbo; and Hans Joachim Bernet, the well-known long-distance driver, were witnesses. We moved into our own new home that same day. It was all unbelievably wonderful—our own home in the magnificent Tessin countryside, with a woman who cared for me, and the peace and quiet I needed to keep me in top shape.

The news of our marriage was like a bomb shell. Nobody had thought that Baby intended to get married again and certainly no one was aware that she and I had plans in that direction.

Three days after the wedding we went to Bremen, on our way to New York where I wanted to participate in the Roosevelt Field race. As we walked along the quay the fellows from Auto-Union and Mercedes were standing at the rail ogling us with field glasses. Also there were the newly married Rosemeyer couple, little von Delius and racing director Dr. Feuereissen, as well as Dick Seaman and Alfred Neubauer. Neubauer was genuinely delighted to see us together.

"I've always thought we should have Madame Hoffmann with us to clock the time over there!" he said. "And now Rudi's simply married her quickly and secretly and brought her along."

Bernd Rosemeyer burst into our cabin early in the morning to present us with a handsome pewter jug as a wedding gift. It was he who eventually won the American race in an Auto-Union, with Seaman in a Mercedes getting second place. I had had the lead at the start but in the end I dropped out because of a damaged supercharger. Life saw to it that my trees didn't grow all the way into the sky! The first prize was $20,000 and how well that would have fitted into the hole the new house had torn into my pocket.

"Well, that boy can use the money very well too," said Baby. "He's got a new household too and needs lots of things."

Afterward I won the Grand Prix of Germany, Switzerland, Czechoslovakia, and the first run on the Avus. Then two second places and four honorable mentions.

I became European champion, German champion and a husband—all in that important, happy year of 1937.

They were working under high pressure in the factories. The thoroughly trained minds of technicians and inventors were pushed to their greatest efforts. The fever spread through the entire production process, and in the testing labs of Untertuer-kheim the lights were on all night.

Early in January 1938 I got a letter from them. The new car, built for speed records, was ready. It was to be tried out on the autobahn between Frankfurt and Darmstadt.

Until then Rosemeyer, in an Auto-Union, held the top speed record of 400 kilometers per hour—we were going to try to break it.

The record run was scheduled for early morning January 28.

It was still dark when I arrived. The moon stood like a sickle over the little pine wood at the starting line. Hoarfrost lay over everything. The road was absolutely white, and the pines shimmered in the moonlight.

I could spot the starting place from afar. Lights were moving to and fro. When I drove up I could hear Neubauer's loud voice, ordering the mechanics about. They were marking off the section of the road for the run.

I got out of the car and went over to the men gathered in a little black cluster on the white road. There were Director Sailer, who was the chief engineer, Neubauer and Brauchitsch. All three were wrapped in heavy coats. It was very cold, so cold that a cloud of vapor accompanied every word. We said hello.

"Well, how does it look?"

Sailer pointed to the record-breaking car.

"Good, we hope."

There stood the car, enormous, hugging the ground, a crouching monster on four wheels. The bright silvery paint looked strangely pale in the morning light. I walked around it, giving it the once-over. The wheels seemed to have disappeared into the body; it looked like a white whale. It was impossible to take a corner with this armored beast. It could only shoot straight ahead like a projectile.

I got into my touring car and drove down the stretch with Brauchitsch. We drove very slowly. I looked up at the tops of the pines. They stirred in the morning breeze—but just faintly, sleepily. So there was no danger from the wind. However, the road was slippery. The one side that was in the shadow of the pines was covered with hoarfrost. I could drive on the dry side, but with that car I needed the entire width of road.

I decided to wait for the hoarfrost to thaw; to start earlier would be an insane risk. We got back to the starting place and Neubauer came over.

"When do you want to start, Rudi?"

"When it gets light enough and the hoarfrost is gone."

To keep warm we trotted up and down the road. Gradually the sky turned light in the east. It became green as grass, then pink. The naked, black branches of the trees stood out sharply like skeletons before the brightening horizon. Then the sun slowly pushed up over the ridge of the Taunus Mountains. A swarm of crows flew out of the pine woods and over the empty fields, toward the town that was lying in the morning mist, hazy blue and very far away.

By eight o'clock the frost had evaporated. I climbed into the car.

"Go!" Neubauer commanded. The mechanics pushed the car, running alongside until the motor started. Then they stayed behind and I was off. The shift worked wonderfully easy, the car hugged the road beautifully—I was aware of that even on the starting run. It drove altogether differently from the car they had the year before.

I put on speed, and more speed. The road before me seemed to shrink, becoming narrower and narrower, till it was a slender, white ribbon. The trees on either side merged into a solid black wall.

The flag—the finish. . . . I let the car roll and come to a stop.

The mechanics came running up, shouting and waving their arms. Their voices sounded strangely thin and tinny in the morning silence. Every single one of them shook my hand.

For the length of a cigarette I did nothing, greedily inhaling the smoke, awaiting tensely what news the telephone would bring. Meanwhile the mechanics turned the car around and made ready to start for the run back. Only the average speed of the run back and forth was counted as the official record.

At last a man came running up.

"It's a record, Mr. Caracciola!" he shouted; "average of 427 kilometers per hour!" (265 m.p.h.)

I waved him my thanks and then I was off again. This time

I stepped harder on the gas, right from the beginning. A wind had sprung up, just a faint morning breeze, but I could feel it trying to push the car to the right while I bucked it with the wheel.

Again the road constricted to a narrow, white band with overpasses that seemed like small, black holes, and at the speed I was going I had to steer accurately to pass through them. But even before the brain quite grasped what was to be done, the car had already streaked on.

I couldn't understand that my brain should be slower than the speed of my car. Again and again I had that strange impression that I had to aim in order to get through.

Out in the open there was again the struggle against the resisting air currents. Then, the starting line once more—the flag. I took my foot off the gas but I could not brake. The rubber on the tires was so thin that the slightest braking pressure would have ripped them and the result would have been unthinkable.

So I let the car roll for almost three kilometers and then I was back where I had started. Neubauer was the first at the car, beaming and shouting excitedly:

"Four thirty-seven, Rudi. Record!" (271 m.p.h.)

He spread his arms, wanting to embrace me but he couldn't reach me—the car was too wide.

"You want to do one more?"

I shook my head, no.

Surrounding the car I saw happy, laughing faces, waving hands. They were all there, my friends, my helpers. I couldn't hear much in my capsule and I still had wax in my ears. Then they unscrewed the top. Air—how marvelous this fresh, cool air and how wonderful that we had made it, my car and I! They pushed a ladder across the side of the car and I climbed out of the seat and down the ladder directly into the arms of the jubilant crowd that shared my happiness over this success.

"Bravo, Rudi!" Neubauer shouted, embracing me. "437

kilometers in the one direction—432.692 kilometers average both ways."

"The car drives beautifully," I said. "But you can get even more out of it. We ought to do it again tomorrow with a higher rear axle ratio."

Briefly we discussed the run once more, then I walked over to my wife who was waiting for me in the car. For seconds we remained in a close embrace, not speaking. She always waited for me at the pit or our own car, until the car and the crowd had released me and she could claim me once more.

Our car was warm and cozy, a bit like a small home on wheels. It almost seemed to me now as if that flight in the beautiful silver monster had been a dream. How ever did I get through those tiny, black holes . . .?

Our car was surrounded by reporters and people waiting to congratulate me, most of them old friends. They wanted me to tell them about it. What could I say? That the car drove well and that I had never thought a road could look so narrow; and, yes, surely I'd make it even faster the next day if all went well.

In one long queue of cars we drove back to the Park Hotel for breakfast at leisure and in peace. The peace was of short duration. Neubauer was called to the telephone and came back to the table in a state of high excitement.

"The Auto-Union gang is out there! With their record car. With Rosemeyer and the whole bunch. They're on their way to the autobahn. Come on, hurry, we've got to be there. I'm sure they want to smash our record before the noon edition. How do you like that?"

It was a sensation. We were speechless. Who ever heard of records being run like races? It was murder.

"I'm not going out there," I said.

For a second I could see it like a vivid picture: two armored monsters racing against each other until one of them was vanquished. And besides, it was too late in the day now; the air wasn't calm enough any more. Even during the morning I had felt the breeze coming through the trees. At that speed the tires barely touched the ground and you could feel the faintest whiff of air.

The first excitement died down. We all fell silent. Our thoughts were out there, at the Autobahn Frankfurt-Darmstadt. After breakfast, while we were smoking, Brauchitsch asked:

"Don't you think perhaps we should, after all . . .?"

"Yes," I said. "We might as well go there because we can't be at peace here."

We drove out again. This time the starting place was black with people. Reporters were there, sports enthusiasts, spectators. A great number of cars stood parked on both sides along the Autobahn. The sky was partly overcast, with scuds of clouds drifting over the fields, while some parts of the landscape lay in bright sunlight. The wind had increased and, in driving along, I noticed how restlessly the tree tops were moving.

When we arrived Rosemeyer was already sitting in his car, surrounded by a crowd. I pushed my way through and held out my hand to him.

"Congratulations, Rudi," he said and smiled, his white teeth flashing.

"Thank you," I said. I wanted to say something more, too, a lot more. All rivalry was forgotten at that moment. He was my comrade, exposed to the same dangers as I.

I saw him sitting there ready to start and I felt a momentary dread. I wanted to tell him that it was perhaps too windy, that he should try it in the early morning instead. When I myself had sat behind the steering wheel I had thought only of the task—now I thought only of the danger. My throat tightened—I could not, I must not tell him anything. . . .

Once again he laughed at me, his boyish, happy laughter. Then he turned toward somebody else. I went back to my car and sat down behind the steering wheel. We were sitting there as in a small, warm room under the open sky. Brauchitsch was next to me.

"In that wind!" I said. "Can you understand that?"

He shrugged.

Then we saw the people at the line-up breaking away and Rosemeyer's car shot off like a white arrow. The crowd gathered back into a black clump, awaiting his return.

In a little while Rosemeyer was back; he had made better time than the previous year but not enough to break my record.

The wind had become even stronger. Once more Rosemeyer got ready for the start. And then he was off on the second run. We sat in the car and waited—waited. . . .

Suddenly there was a movement among the crowd. A few people began running down the road, then they were all running. I rolled down the car window.

"What's happened?" I shouted at a boy who was running by.

"Rosemeyer has crashed," he shouted back and ran on.

We remained behind alone.

"I don't want to go there," I said.

"Neither do I," Brauchitsch muttered. And, after a while, he added: "Why? Was this necessary?"

I didn't answer but I felt as if I were staring into an abyss that had suddenly opened up. Indeed, why? What was the sense in men chasing each other to death for the sake of a few seconds? To serve progress? To serve mankind? What a ridiculous phrase in the face of the great reality of death. But then—why? Why?

And for the first time, at that moment, I felt that every life is lived according to its own laws. And that the law for a fighter is: to burn oneself up to the last fiber, no matter what happens to the ashes.

One solitary figure came walking in our direction. Dr.Glaeser, the medical official for the Mercedes and Auto-Union teams. His face was solemn. He stepped up to our car.

"Dead!" he said. "He's lying on his back in the woods, staring into the sky, and he looks as if he's still breathing."

I pressed my lips together. At that instant I felt as if all life had stopped.

Our hearts were congealed. It was inevitable—how could anyone survive an accident at that speed? But we had hoped for a miracle. So had he, too—Bernd Rosemeyer, the personification of youth, of heroic courage. Smiling, as if it were sheer play, he had won his victories. And yet he too had to pay for them and fate had demanded the highest payment of all from him. I would never forget him, Rosemeyer, my comrade.

Dr. Glaeser remained standing by the car, his head bowed. I shook his hand. I shivered. Turning the car, we drove back into town.

20

As I write this, it is the year 1958 and since those fateful days twenty years have gone by. The gap Rosemeyer left behind has never been closed.

A few months ago, on the twentieth anniversary of Rosemeyer's death, a memorial service was held at the scene of the accident. I went to Frankfurt to take part in the service and I laid a wreath with the silver-blue Mercedes ribbon before the stone memorial. I imagined him with us again, the slim blond boy, laughing and joking in his customary fashion. Since we belonged to competing stables we had not often been together, but we had frequently laughed or even quarreled together, the latter only briefly and rarely.

In that hellish tempo we imposed on each other everything was mercilessly hard. We did not give a second to each other. It was his wild, stormy youth against the experience of an opponent ten years older. I was thirty-seven then, Rosemeyer twenty-seven. He wanted to push me off my throne, whereas I wanted to sit there a while longer, at least until a new generation of racing drivers came along.

Lang was already there—he had been driving with us during practice for several years, and then was given the reserve car during the races. Seaman, too, was a comer who had won many races on smaller cars. Of the younger men Rosemeyer was the most daring and without doubt a natural. He did not know fear, and sometimes that is not good. You had to know where the real danger lay.

We actually feared for his life in every race. Somehow I didn't think that a long life was in the cards for him. It was bound to get him sooner or later. But to reach his end during a speed record run was something nobody had expected.

Many friends and admirers of Rosemeyer appeared for that memorial service, including an American delegation from a sports car club, with a magnificent wreath. A few speeches were made in praise of Rosemeyer's courage and incredible talent. Elly Beinhorn-Rosemeyer had come with her son, and once again relived the tragic hour of loss of the husband she had loved so much. How hard the years afterward must have been for her! But she rebuilt her life courageously, centering it all around her young son Bernd.

Now Bernd was grown up, a slender, blond young man like his father. I brought up the subject of car racing.

"No," he said quietly and smiled. "I don't want to become a racing driver. I am going to be a doctor."

Elly Beinhorn-Rosemeyer regarded her son lovingly. A doctor! Yes, thank God, not a racing driver, was perhaps what she was thinking. And in my memory I see her, the famous girl pilot Elly Beinhorn-Rosemeyer walking upright and controlled behind the coffin of her husband. Rosemeyer had been honored with a state funeral in Berlin. All of us colleagues and racing drivers in our racing overalls had escorted him to his final resting place.

The music, the muffled drums accompanied our slow steps. The monotonous rhythm penetrated our hearts and translated itself into words: *You today and I tomorrow, you today and I tomorrow. . . .*"

Everything inside me had rebelled for a moment. Was this our purpose in life? Reckless devotion to a great aim, a few days of glory and then a gruesome death?

The drums continued beating ominously. I told myself to stop thinking. *He* no longer felt anything—for *him* it was over, whatever it was we were facing.

They lowered him into the grave. Adieu, comrade, adieu to a glorious young challenger!

Life went on. We, the drivers of Auto-Union and Mercedes went back to our working places. The racing program of 1938 left us little time for brooding or mourning one of our number.

The races were becoming faster and harder all the time and the number of potential winners was increasing. There was Hermann Lang, Manfred von Brauchitsch, Luigi Fagioli, Hasse, H. P. Mueller, Gigi Villoresi, Hans Stuck, Tazio Nuvolari, Guiseppe Farina, Dick Seaman, Count Didi Trossi, Achille Varzi, Piero Taruffi, J. P. Wimille, Louis Chiron, René Dreyfus, Raymond Sommer. With opponents of that caliber you might stay among the leaders, but only one could be first; and to be first in such a talented crowd was a great accomplishment.

Our new 3-liter racing cars with superchargers could reach, with proper gears, about 330 kilometers (105 mph.). Under the guidance of the two chief construction engineers Wagner and Max Sailer, Daimler-Benz had created a new top product for the new racing formula—a 3-liter, 12-cylinder engine that had 450 hp.

The first race that year was in Pau, in southern France. It went for a hundred torturous laps and we suffered defeat. Lang and I were assigned as Mercedes drivers, with Seaman standing by in reserve—much to his distaste. It started off badly. During training we noticed that the course was bad for our gasoline-devouring supercharged motors. Then, to make things worse, Lang's brakes went wrong the last day of practice. He skidded and hit a fence with the back of the car, damaging the chassis. In spite of hasty repairs by the mechanics the car was not ready for the start.

So it turned out that I alone had to try to cope with René

Dreyfus. He was in the lead at the beginning. Too soon I had to pull up for gasoline. Since Dreyfus, with his compressor-less Delahaye "bathtub" didn't have to gas up, he had the race won from that moment on. What was the point in brooding over it?—besides, René was happy, and anyhow, after the ill-fated (for us) race in Pau came Tripolis. There it was our turn again—Brauchitsch's, Lang's and mine.

Tripolis was a great experience every time in spite of the heat, the gagging dust-fine yellow sand and the voracious mosquitoes. And flies! Our pet monkey Anatol liked to eat flies, but not in Tripolis for some reason, perhaps because they tasted of camel, just as most of the bazaar goods smelled of camel.

We enjoyed the luxurious, cool hotel lobby when we came back from practice. I never went outside, but Baby used every free moment to roam the narrow streets in the old town, admiring the marvelous cloth and silverware. Of course, she always found something to buy. During those forays of hers we men, Anatol and I, slept.

On the day of the race the Arabs gathered all along the track. Shrouded in white woolen barracans they did not feel the sand and the fierce sun.

Italo Balbo, the creator of this beautiful fairytale city of Tripolis, was to start us off. We had to warm up the motors several times—the marshal was late. Finally we were off. During the first lap we felt as if we were driving blind through a yellow-gray wall of dust. A sandstorm was blowing from the desert and the wheels of the cars whirled up the sand that lay in the road like snow. The fine grains of sand burned like a thousand needles on the skin. It got into the teeth and dried out the mouth. Soon the little windshield looked as if it had been wiped with sandpaper.

It was a triple Mercedes victory with Lang the victor, Brauchitsch and I following closely after him. Then came Sommer in his Alfa-Romeo and Dreyfus with his Delahaye.

In the evening the usual magnificent ball was scheduled in the marshal's palace. But the ball was canceled—we could not celebrate. Death had reaped a rich harvest on that dreadful day. In the ninth lap Siena with the 12-cylinder Alfa-Romeo crashed fatally. He was trying in vain to pass Cortese on the little 1½-liter Alfa and his car smashed into an Arab house and crushed Siena underneath. Not knowing that he had been an obstacle for the other car, Cortese went on.

In the thirteenth lap there was another awful accident. At a speed of over 200 kilometers the cars of Farina and Lazlo Hartmann collided. The desert wind must have pushed Farina's car to one side so that he grazed Hartmann's Maserati. Both cars turned over and the drivers were thrown into the road like lifeless rag dolls. In that second I came racing up—by a sheer miracle I managed to drive through the whirling debris, just missing the two figures on the ground. I felt a tingling like an electric shock, all the way to my finger tips. That, I thought, is what they mean by a thrill of horror.

When I came around again the bodies were gone. The wreckage had been moved aside. Each time I passed I tried to read the numbers, but the cars were so badly smashed that I couldn't make them out.

Later, I learned Siena, the popular Italian racing driver, who like so many others had grown up on a motorcyle, had been killed. Hartmann, too, died of a severe spine injury. Farina had suffered a concussion and facial injuries. Heavy and light racing cars should not be allowed to start together. Siena, in coming around a bend at full speed, had come upon Cortese who was driving more slowly and could not swerve past him. It may be that the Farina-Hartmann accident was caused by similar circumstances. Hartmann was a lovable fellow, but he frequently got in the way of the fast cars.

After each accident they look for new safety measures, but death finds ever new ways to catch his victims.

21

Richard Beattie Seaman, the young Mercedes racing driver, won the Grand Prix of Germany in 1938. I had eaten rotten fish or something the day before the race and had an upset stomach. From one lap to the next it kept getting worse. Then, when I saw Lang standing alongside his car at the pits, I stopped, gave him my car, and he came in second.

Actually Manfred von Brauchitsch should have been the winner of this race. He had led most of the way, followed closely—too closely—by Seaman, who drove with icy calm. While refilling his tank, Manfred looking purple and quite upset had shouted:

"Neubauer, that Seaman is driving me insane! He drives up so close, each time I brake I think, Now we'll crash! We'll both end up in the ditch if this keeps up."

Neubauer ran over to Seaman who had just pulled up for refilling.

"Seaman," he said, "leave Brauchitsch alone; don't chase him. You're endangering our double victory. The competition is out, so there's no use putting on a private race that might cost us our victory."

Seaman was silent.

Meanwhile gasoline had run over the red-hot exhaust pipe of Brauchitsch's car. As the engine started, a spark was thrown up and within seconds the air was rent violently—and flames shot up. The car was a conflagration, the flames at least twenty feet high. Horrified, Manfred, in an effort to escape, yanked at the steering wheel until it came loose. He was enveloped in flames, his suit, his gloves were burning, yet he was helpless to do anything but wave his arms.

But there was Neubauer, the Big One. Heedless of the fire or danger of explosion, he fell upon the car with the courage of a lion, tore and clawed the blond giant out of his seat, beat the flames off his driving cap, rolled him on the ground until the flames were extinguished.

The mechanics, working on the car with fire extinguishers, soon had the fire out. A catastrophe had been prevented.

An amusing note was not lacking. You could have skied in front of the pit; everybody at hand was wiping foam from clothes and faces. Manfred prepared to get back into his car, and the public cheered him wildly. Neubauer wiped his sweaty face and took a deep breath—but his mouth remained open. Seaman's car, which had been ready to take off for many seconds, was still standing.

"God, is the man out of his mind?" Neubauer roared. "Go on, take off! Why aren't you taking off?" In a white rage he ran over to Seaman. "Go on, Seaman, take off!" he shouted.

"You said not to chase Brauchitsch," Seaman replied, utterly calm.

"Well, for God's sake, Seaman, do you really want to cost us our victory? What shall I do? What do you want? I promise you, I make a holy vow, that you won't be chased either if we're ahead at the Grand Prix of England."

Seaman adjusted his goggles and, without a look or a word, drove off, and his car disappeared with a roar toward the south curve. Brauchitsch meanwhile had wiped the foam off the steering wheel, pulled on another pair of gloves and waited, trembling, for the motor to be started with the electric starter. Impatiently he jammed the steering wheel into place. Amid a roar of applause he raced after Seaman. Manfred, the "Unlucky One," . . . again he did justice to his nickname. Out near the airport he suddenly found himself with his steering wheel loose in his hands. Alertly he grabbed the steering spindle with both hands and, holding desperately, carefully guided the braking car into a shallow ditch.

It was over.

A track attendant drove over to the road along the track, near the stands, and soon Manfred appeared in sight, on foot, carrying his steering wheel. The public greeted him with a great shout of sympathy. Manfred was indeed the man of the day.

I went over to him and patted him on the shoulder.

"Manfred, old boy," I said, "that's the way it goes. Up one day and down the next. Another day it'll be different."

Manfred turned away. He had a red face again, only this time he was close to tears. What he said in reply had better not be repeated.

Dick Seaman had won his first Grand Prix of Germany.

When we returned to the Hotel Eifeler Hof in Adenau that evening, Manfred was nowhere to be seen.

"Go see what the boy is doing," I told my wife. Baby went on tiptoe over to the next room and there the big fellow was, stretched out on the bed and sobbing with anger and disappointment. Baby sat on the edge of his bed and ran her hand over his tousled head and I sat down on a chair. We let him give vent to his feelings and then I ordered an enormous jug of cold orange juice. After a warm bath there remained only the victory celebration to be gotten over with a smile. In the morning the fellow with the proverbial bad luck would be over the worst of his grief.

In the center of the long table sat Dick Seaman, the trophy in front of him. Next to him sat Erika Popp, daughter of the director general of the BMW works. I had the impression

Charles Faroux, veteran French sports writer and racing expert, was the starter at all great European racing events. Here he is preparing the start at the Monaco Grand Prix 1937. Caracciola is in No. 8 at the left.

Caracciola at full speed in the Monaco Grand Prix of 1937.

Caracciola with Bernd Rosemeyer, at the
pits in Bern, 1938.

Caracciola at the pits during the race, changing plugs and refilling.

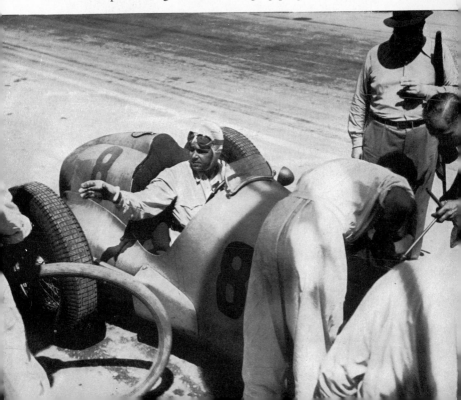

Rudi Caracciola in 1938.

Caracciola driving to victory at Pescara, Italy, in 1938, as Neubauer waves him in.

Caracciola in the Record car on the Frankfurt-Darmstadt Autobahn in 1938.

Mercedes-Benz racing cars of 1939: *left*, the 3-liter supercharged racing car, formula 1938–40; *right*, the new 1½-liter supercharged racing car built for the Lottery Race in

Caracciola in the 3-liter 12-cylinder Mercedes-Benz Record car at Dessau.

Record driving on the highway at Dessau, in February, 1939.

Rudolf and Alice Caracciola after his victory in the German Grand Prix, 1939, on the Nuerburgring.

Left to right: Floyd Clymer, American publisher and authority on racing cars, Anton Hulman, Jr., President of the Indianapolis Motor Speedway Corporation, and Leonard Marshall, Secretary of the Speedway Management (1946).

Caracciola with the Mercedes Roadster 300 SL in the spring of 1959.

Rudolf Caracciola with Karl Kling and Hermann Lang, before the Mille Miglia Race in Italy in 1952. The car is the Mercedes Sports Car 300 SL.

Caracciola with General F. F. Everest and Major C. R. Clark of the United States Air Force, explaining some details of the 300 SL Mercedes Sportscar.

Caracciola's accident during training on the Indianapolis Motor Speedway in May, 1946. The racing car was a Thorne Engineering Special, six-cylinder with one carburetor per cylinder.

Caracciola's accident in Bern, Switzerland, in May, 1952.

Caracciola's trophy room.

Rudolf Caracciola at home with his wife, Alice, and their cat, Tessa, in the summer of 1958.

Memorial service held for Rudolf Caracciola at the Daimler-Benz factory in Stuttgart-Untertuerkheim in 1959. The ceremony took place on the trial grounds, where Caracciola had been driving a pre-war racing car for a TV demonstration a month before.

Bust of Caracciola in gold bronze by Swedish sculptor Hedblom, at the cemetery of Castagnola in Lugano.

that Dick had won a double victory that day. It was most charming to see the two of them exchanging glances time and again. Erika was seventeen, Dick twenty-five. If it had not been for the political tensions I'd have sworn they would be a pair soon.

From the Nuerburgring we went to Lugano and shortly afterward on to Pescara to the race for the Coppa Acerbo. We went to the Adriatic, via Milan, Modena, Bologna and Rimini, and then down the long straight road beside the foaming sea to Pescara. In the villages the people sat in front of their doors, on low chairs, their backs turned to the road. Children ran back and forth; dogs, donkey carts and innumerable bicyclists crowded the streets. The safest way to drive under those circumstances was with hand on horn, constantly. The landscape was lovely but we had little time to enjoy it. This evening we had to be in Pescara and the distance from Lugano was 750 kilometers. We drove without stopping, at one stretch. We would eat in the evening, and we carried fruit to quench our thirst.

We reached Pescara in the evening. Many members of our racing "family" had already arrived before us. We were staying at the new luxury hotel by the sea. From the outside it looked luxurious indeed, but that was a somewhat misleading impression. Since the hotel had had to be finished in great haste for the start of the race, many things were only makeshift, such as the sanitary installations. The mosquitoes arrived early. In fact, they seemed to have been lying in wait.

Baby had brought along the flowered netting she had bought in the bazaars of Tripolis. As soon as she had unpacked she started screening me in, just as she did in Tripolis. I stretched out on the bed and swatted and chased away any mosquito that was near while she pulled the netting from the head to the foot of the bed and nailed it secure with thumb tacks. And all this amid bursts of laughter.

"Rudi, if you could only see yourself—just like a piece of plum pie under a fly screen!"

I didn't think it funny at all. It was depressing enough to sleep under a mosquito net, but under this thing, that was stretched across me only an inch or so away, I barely got air enough to breathe. However, I had to endure it. In Tripolis, Pescara and Livorno I was always packed away under the flowered net because otherwise the mosquitoes would bite my hands, which then swelled up so that I could not even pull on my gloves the next day.

The Pescara race track is 25 kilometers long. One part of it is a marvelous, curved mountain road and the other an endlessly long straightaway that leads partly along the sea. This year they had built in two chicanes on the long straightaway in order to cut down the speed there. Chicanes are artificially built corners that lead off the track and then back on it.

The Italian cars were fast and maneuverable, but our Mercedes and Auto-Union cars were considerably faster in the stretches. Thus we were always on the lookout for new ways of evening out the chances of the various cars. Without these chicanes the Italian car would have had hardly a chance of winning. They had to make victory more difficult for the German cars in order to arouse public interest.

Technically speaking, preparing the cars for Pescara created many headaches. The serpentine road demanded a lower gear and heavily treaded tires. The long straightaway, on the other hand, practically called for high gear and smooth tires. So a golden mean had to be found that would do on both roads but would not be entirely satisfactory on either

After the hours of practice we all sat down together for a tactical conference. Each driver contributed his own ideas. I think these occasions were Neubauer's favorite ones. Like a general he sat ensconced among his soldiers, or rather like a good shepherd among his flock. Looking back, I suppose he was mainly the good shepherd, one whose voice could be heard from far away. As a matter of fact, when Neubauer, Brauchitsch and I thought we were merely conversing the walls would almost collapse; we had, all three of us, the voices of field commanders during battle.

"So, listen here, Caracciola!" . . . "Look, pay some attention, Manfred, stop thinking of all those girls!" . . . "Lang, you're not even listening when I talk to you!" . . . "Quiet, everybody here's what we'll do. . . ."

And then all preparations were discussed in detail.

During practice I tried out various driving methods. After doing a few laps, I worked out a scheme of my own for the race. I had to save the motor on the straightaway so it wouldn't turn sour and I'd have to gain back the seconds this would cost me in the mountains. Boy oh boy, what a race it was going to be! And how those brakes would suffer when we had to hold down to zero before those chicanes.

Shortly after nine A.M. the cars were pushed to their starting positions in the line-up. It was already hot; an oppressive, humid heat.

The red, blue and silver-white cars made a colorful, festive picture. The stands were filled to the rafters. Little boys with curly black hair had climbed up the iron poles supporting the stands for a better view. You could almost feel the enthusiasm and suspense of the sports-minded crowd. Of course they hoped for the victory of one of the red Italian cars, but they would applaud the performance of the foreign drivers just as sincerely.

About one minute before the race the motors were turned up and the cars started a concerted roar. The spectators could easily distinguish between the sounds of the different makes. We had the highest, most metallic tone; it practically rent the air. I was conscious of no other sound except a dull drone inside my skull. My ears, like those of all other drivers, were stopped with wads of wax to prevent injury to the ear drums. Even then it sometimes took hours before we could hear normally again.

The start was always the most exciting part and every driver coped with the tension in his own way. Nuvolari was like a racehorse, almost unable to control his temper until the flag came down. Brauchitsch pressed his lips together and gave an impression of tight suspense. Lang was outwardly very calm.

We were off. Brauchitsch took off like a rocket—magnificently. I raced past Nuvolari as fast as I could and then I held within a distance of seconds behind Manfred. For three laps we trailed each other closely; then I saw a cloud of smoke shooting up from Manfred's car.

I thought, he's had it!

And so it was. Manfred slowed down, then signaled me to pass. Now it was my turn. Lang followed close on my heels. I stepped on the gas a little. Record lap. The motor was humming contentedly. Record in eleven minutes—that made an average of 140.640 kilometers. On the straightaway they clocked the flying start which, in my car, came to 276.923 km.p.h. Brauchitsch had dropped out. Now Didi Trossi in his Maserati was slowly drawing ahead. The sign from the pit informed me that he had passed Farina and was now in third place behind Lang.

He could become dangerous. I had to secure a bigger lead, otherwise he would get me when I had to refuel. Didi Trossi hit a wall and injured his arm. In spite of great pain he brought his car to the pit and Villoresi, whose car had given up the ghost, took over Trossi's car. The stormy Gigi raced a lap that took everyone's breath away. With 10.57 he made it three seconds faster than I.

I thought, I hope he can keep this up. . . .

He couldn't. Villoresi's motor gave up.

With all this chasing I relinquished my famed "exemplary" driving style and now I was tearing around the mountain curves like a maniac. The stones scattered. Zigzagging, I skidded over the curves. Only thus could I afford to let up on the gas a little on the straightaway, to give the engine a chance to recover.

Now the sign said Nuvolari out of the race. Later I heard that he had to give up because of engine failure.

Lang was no longer behind me. Beyond the first chicane I saw fire. A car was ablaze. I drove close to the wooden fence of the chicane to avoid the long, hissing flames. It was a Mercedes—Lang's. He was not in his car, thank God!—I could see through the smoke. It looked like a terrible fire. There was nothing left to extinguish, that I could see. The car would burn up completely with 200 liters of gasoline and the tank would explode.

The fuel was highly explosive—we called it dynamite. When our cars started before the pit in order to warm the motors, people had to run from the pits. The sharp fumes got into the lungs, smarted the eyes, and anyhow it wasn't exactly safe to be close to that fuel in action. If a fire started for some reason, it took a while for the flames to come. At first the air over the hood would tremble and shimmer and the heat would become unbearable; then came the fire. Lang had recognized the trembling air and had jumped from the car before he got singed.

In the following laps the acrid odor of burning rubber was noticeable from far away. Slowly the flames subsided and the fire began to eat away at the skeleton of the car. It smoldered for hours after the race—a hideous heap of twisted, red-hot metal.

The sign announced Mueller's Auto-Union second with a distance of 2 kilometers. Later Mueller too dropped out; I was the only German, the only one of our team left in the race. Whenever I came around Neubauer was standing almost in the center of the track. From far away I saw him raising his hands and signaling with the flag, as if to say, slowly, slowly, dear Rudi—only you can save the day!

I nodded, waved a thank-you and then the last lap was done. I thought my heart would burst with joy. The strategy had been correct then, and the goddess Fortuna had been riding with us from the start. Victory! It was mine alone!

As always, Neubauer was the first arrival at the car. He hugged me, and in that hug there was gratitude, friendship, and admiration for my performance. Then they were all around me and the people almost crushed me. Here they were, all who made the victory possible—dear old Walz, Zimmer, Lindemeyer, Grupp, Bunz, Mueller, Woerner and the other mechanics. There was the master, the great, unforgettable master Dietrich with the Kaiser Wilhelm mustache, the tire specialist of the Continental Racing Service. There were the Bosch specialists, Bamminger foremost among them. Also there was Eberhard Hundt, the well-known sports reporter, who followed the races with enthusiasm and described them with technical accuracy. Beside him was Fabian, the reporter from the *Berliner Zeitung*. And finally, there was my own little woman, our timekeeper, thanks to whom we knew how we stood in the race and whatever else was going on around the track. Now she stopped the second hand of her stop watch, rolled up her racing sheet, and was beaming because I had come through with no bones broken.

The spectators had broken through the lines and we stood in an impenetrable crowd. It took a long time before we could get out and return to the hotel. The press photographers tried to get a presentable picture out of my oil-blackened face.

The Grand Prix of Switzerland was to take place exactly a week later and for that reason I wanted to get home as quickly as possible, out of this heat, in order to put my tortured leg to pasture in the sun. Immediately after the victory dinner I wanted to take off. Baby didn't know that yet. I was lying in the bathtub trying to get rid of the smell of oil and gasoline. Baby had put out the dark suit for me and was ironing a dinner gown for the victory celebration. How was I to tell her that this was going to be a very long night. . . .

"Baby," I said, gently as possible. "Little one, you might start to pack. We are going home tonight."

"To Lugano, tonight!" she exclaimed. "Are you mad?"

"No," I said. "We'll sneak off after dinner. We'll take Manfred along, and he can drive part of the way."

Baby said nothing further. During the racing season I was the absolute dictator—she knew that I had to lie down as much as possible between races and that, after a race, I wanted to hear no more about races or driving or motors. So she took a headache powder and proceeded to pack. She folded the sleeping-beauty flowered-tulle, put the thumbtacks into a special box, and made a special package of the racing coveralls along with the oil-stained, well-worn racing shoes. The penetrating odor of oil and gasoline would always cling to them. Without those shoes I'm sure I would not be myself. Most drivers feel that way. The shoes knew the foot—they were intimate with the foot pedals, exactly fitting into the narrow space. Racing shoes were guarded like holy relics.

After dinner we changed. I went downstairs, paid the bill and stashed away the bags. The porter was shaking his head. To drive through the night after such a race!

Manfred took the wheel as far as Bologna, then I drove on to Lugano. Moritz, our dachshund, welcomed us with joy until his breath gave out, and the tiny monkey Anatol greeted him with excited chatter. We were happiest of all; to be home, in our own beds. Only Manfred found something to gripe about—in the morning Anatol robbed him of half his breakfast egg.

22

On Wednesday morning we started off to Bern for the Grand Prix. The course is outside the town, in a park with magnificent old trees. It is about seven kilometers long, with a short straightaway before the stands, with cobblestones and fast, flat curves. The entire course becomes very slippery when it rains.

Thursday practice began. The weather was unfriendly and it did not improve in the following days. It seemed to be getting ready for a cloudburst on Sunday.

Since our practice laps were the fastest, we Mercedes drivers were in the front row. For a while we just stood around. It was raining lightly. The cars were covered and Walz held an umbrella over me so I wouldn't get soaked before the race had even started. Just before three we got into the cars, fastened the mica rain protector over the crash helmet; beneath that we wore the usual racing goggles.

We put the goggles on only a few seconds before the start so the glasses wouldn't steam up. Our starting positions looked like this:

Caracciola	Lang	Seaman
Mercedes	Mercedes	Mercedes
v. Brauchitsch	Stuck	
Mercedes	Auto-Union	

Wimille	Nuvolari	H. P. Mueller
Alfa-Romeo	Auto-Union	Auto-Union

Farina	Kautz
Alfa-Romeo	Auto-Union

Teagno	Dreyfus	Taruffi
Maserati	Delahaye	Alfa-Romeo

Raph
Delahaye

Mandirola	Christen	Romano
Maserati	Maserati	Alfa-Romeo

de Sztriha	Minozzi
Alfa-Romeo	Alpha-Romeo

We started at three. Seaman, coming from the far right, shot into the lead. He was followed by Stuck, then me, then Mueller, Kautz, Brauchitsch, Nuvolari—who was driving his first Auto-Union car—Lang, Farina, Taruffi, Wimille and the others. On the fourth lap I passed Stuck. Seaman drove brilliantly. He was still in the lead on the eighth lap. Now it was raining harder . . . it was pouring. A cloudburst. Just behind Seaman, I drove as if in a water fountain. His wheels threw the water and the dirt of the street into my windshield. In order to see, I had to stick my head out to the side and then I had that much more sludge in my face and on my goggles.

Enough of that, I thought. Watch it, Dick, because now it's my turn to take the lead!

Next to the Nuerburgring, Bern is my favorite circuit. Dick fought back as hard as he could—but I could do it faster and finally I overtook him through dirt and water on the slippery cobblestones.

Seaman tried to follow me, but when I put on speed the geysers thrown back by my wheels were higher too The water rose behind me like a wall. I could no longer see Seaman's car in the rear-view mirror. Passing the cars along the course was laborious and dangerous and it seemed to me as if I did nothing but pass other cars. What weather! With the heat pouring over me from the motor I felt as if I were in a steam bath. The rain had softened the ground in the woods and rivulets ran to the road and flowed across the track. I watched like a lynx to catch any change in the surface of the road. Baby said I had the eyes of a seal because I could see so well in the rain. But on a slippery road you must have the right feeling for the car. The car wants to act like a wild horse on the cobblestones. I had to guess what it intended doing before it was done and then I had to control it with calm, gentle motions. It required not only the hands; the entire body was involved in feeling and controlling the car.

Seaman didn't let me steal many seconds from him—I went across the finish line only half a minute ahead of him.

One—two—three, we arrived. Brauchitsch was third. For the third time I'd won the Grand Prix of Switzerland.

Then, on September 11, Nuvolari in an Auto-Union won the Grand Prix of Italy in Monza.

"Nivola," or "Nuff" as we called him, had driven the Auto-Union car for the first time in Bern and by the second start the ever-daring, indestructible master proved that he could also take charge of a car with a rear engine.

However, he had to sit quietly, like a lamb, behind the steering wheel. Surely he was happier on the graceful, maneuverable Alfa-Romeo. He could ride it like a colt, half in the ditch and half on the road, but the car could always be brought back under control. With our cannons you couldn't afford such games—and certainly not with a rear engine.

Except for Bernd Rosemeyer, who had graduated from motorcycles directly to Auto-Union racing cars and who had no basis of comparison with other cars, there was only one who had mastered that vehicle perfectly: Achille Varzi. Our manager, Dr. Feuereissen, and Neubauer once permitted Rosemeyer and me to exchange cars during practice at Monza. It was a sensation: Rosemeyer in a Mercedes and I in an Auto-Union—on the practice cars, of course.

When Rosemeyer got out he said:

"Man, what marvelous brakes you've got! And how that thing hugs the road. . . ."

I said, "a magnificent motor—from lowest to highest speed, and it picks up so smoothly. . . ."

We agreed that the ideal racing car for 1939 should have a Mercedes chassis with Mercedes brakes and Auto-Union engine.

"But," I said, "with the engine in front."

The Grand Prix of Italy was the last Grand Prix race of 1938. The political situation worried all of us. In Italy we were met with some sympathy, but on the whole with outright hostility. War seemed inevitable. However . . . as yet we were still racing and the drivers of many nations participated. It was as hot as only Italy can be in the fall.

It was hot in the cars, even hotter in mine because a gasket had burned out. The heat of the exhaust came directly through the openings of the gas- and gearshift pedals at my feet. In spite of asbestos lining, the gas pedal burned a hole through the leather sole, the asbestos inner sole, right to the sole of my foot—a hole as large as a silver dollar.

Brauchitsch took over from me for a few laps, then he had enough. I got in again, pressing down on the red-hot gas pedal with just the edge of my foot. I was third, after Nuvolari and Farina.

My foot and also my leg hurt so much that I didn't want to participate in the race at Donington, England. Besides, it seemed unlikely that German teams would be welcomed there.

However, the race did take place, because reason seemed to have prevailed in 1938; peace still reigned, though nothing had changed as far as the flaunting of power and military might was concerned. In German racing sport everything is brought to a peak. The organizers were in uniform, the club members were in uniform, and after the race the contingent of uniformed Driver's Corps paraded. At the end of a race we were all tired and sweaty, yet we had to listen to a long patriotic harangue while we stood. If we kept winning, it was the Fatherland that won—if we lost . . . well, that just mustn't happen! The interference with our private lives became unbearable. They were not happy about my living in Lugano. When I settled there, in 1929, it was a happier time, when people could choose their place of residence freely. I had come to Lugano for the first time in 1927 and I liked it as, I suppose, everyone did. It had a mild climate, a lovely landscape and hospitable, friendly people. And—it was situated in the heart of Europe. From there all race tracks were within easy reach.

Since my accident in Monte Carlo in 1933, the southern climate had become vital to me. The hip joint never did heal together properly; muscles and tendons alone supported the leg. That sort of thing is known as a badly healed joint fracture, a wobbly joint. Between races I needed a lot of rest and sun in order to drive 500 kilometers again. Even a sound leg would protest under such a strain.

After a quiet winter, the 1939 racing season began on the 8th of February.

On the newly opened autobahn record track of Dessau-Bitterfeld I was to challenge the existing international class records of the standing and flying kilometer and the standing and flying mile, with the 12-cylinder 2-3 liter Mercedes-Benz model. Furmanik, with a Maserati, held these records then.

In the morning they brought the silver-gray car to the autobahn. In order to reduce the air resistance to a minimum an entirely new streamlined covering of Duralumin had been created which masked the body of the car and the wheels separately. The usual cooler had been left out altogether, the cooling water for the motor came from a refrigerator inside the car. The car was low-slung, extraordinarily beautiful in shape. I could get in comfortably; the seat fitted well. Lindemeyer handed me the steering wheel—I secured it carefully.

With the first trial run I didn't seem to get anywhere. The wheels skidded under me, time and again. There was sand on the new stretch of road. I tried going on the right side of the road which had been used a bit. Now the wheels took, but on this wide road I got no impression of speed.

"Hey, you, Mr. Krauss," I called to our test engineer. "This thing doesn't work. I'm sure it can't go over 300 kilometers." They all broke out in laughter—Neubauer, Sailer, Uhlenhaut and Krauss.

"You did almost 400," said Neubauer. I was speechless. I never would have thought it. Alone on the wide road leading apparently, into infinity, it seemed as if I were airborne. Actually, I was nearly so, because at that speed the contact of wheels to the ground is very slight. At these runs I clocked 177.522 kilometers for the standing kilometer and 204.57 for the standing mile. The flying kilometer I made at 398.230; and the flying mile at 399.560—an inconceivable speed for a 3-liter motor which was, in other words, half as powerful as the 5.7-liter motor I had driven a year earlier on the Frankfurt-Darmstadt autobahn.

The speed runs in Dessau were easier—it meant just letting the car run and correcting it. I didn't have to aim as on the narrow Frankfurt-Darmstadt autobahn with seven overpasses on the stretch. There a millimeter's divergence would have been enough to bring the car in touch with the grass border, which would have been equivalent to a trip to eternity.

From Dessau we drove to the automobile show in Berlin where, afterward, a big honor ceremony was held for the German and European champions in various branches of sport. I was awarded the golden German sports plaque and for the sixth time I was awarded the European championship—three for sports cars, three times for racing cars.

April second another race was held at Pau and we made up for our defeat the previous year. For twenty-nine laps I was in

the lead, ahead of Brauchitsch and Lang. Then it was over—
Fortuna happened to be busy elsewhere. An oil line snapped.
Fixing it cost me seven laps. Then I tried one lap but it didn't
work. My two colleagues won the race and we were all very
satisfied. Brauchitsch turned in the fastest lap.

At the end of May, we found ourselves again in the fairy-tale
country of Libya to take part in another million-lire lottery race.

In order to break the endless victory series of the German
racing cars, the Tripoli Automobile Club specified the race for
1500-cc. racing cars. This was announced in the fall of 1938—
too late for the Germans to build new cars, so they thought.

Here was another opportunity for Daimler-Benz to prove
the ability and working capacity of their designers. Engineers,
mechanics, the entire technical staff all joined with feverish
enthusiasm in the task, and they made possible the seemingly
impossible. Within eight months a 1500 cc. car had been built.

The new car had an 8-cylinder V motor with supercharger,
short wheel-base, five gears, and independent suspension front
and rear.

The short practice run in Hockenheim, before embarking for
Tripolis, turned out satisfactory. The two little cars looked
like offspring of the big ones. The same shape, the same hood.
Graceful, like toys, and so low that, when I stood up, my finger-
tips just touched them.

The news that we were to start in Tripolis after all came as
a total surprise. There were more people than ever gathered in
the stands and the practice speeds promised a fiercely contested
race. Of course, we kept it a complete secret that we had reason
to hope for a top speed of 260 kilometers.

Right after the start Lang took the lead. Neubauer had sent
us into the race with different equipment. Lang started with
worn tires, which he was to change while refilling the tank,
getting another set of worn tires. That way he would have a

faster start—he was to pull the competition after him to wear them out.

I, on the other hand, started with new tires on which I could last through the entire race. During my stop at the pits I was only to refuel. According to the calculations, the time gained thereby would make up for the disadvantage of a start with new tires. However, as happens in life, things turned out entirely different from our expectations. The time it took for my tank to be refilled was longer than refilling and changing tires for Lang's car. The mechanics couldn't find the hole for my electric starter!

Lang won. I was second. Not until ten minutes later did Villoresi in his Alfa-Romeo cross the goal line.

It was an overwhelming success for us—for a new model to have won first and second places in the million-lire race of Tripolis!

After this victory we rushed back to Europe to the Eifel Race on the Nuerburgring which Lang won, ahead of Nuvolari.

On June 25 the Grand Prix of Belgium took place. It is one of the most difficult courses in Europe. Thirty-five laps on a course that is 14½ kilometers long and twists through narrow, tree-lined roads—507 kilometers. Auto-Union, Alfa-Romeo, Maserati and Delahaye were our opponents. The sports-loving King Leopold of Belgium greeted us at the line-up. It was raining. The starting positions were drawn by lot and Neubauer assigned our places: Lang in the first row, Caracciola in the second, Seaman third, Brauchitsch fourth.

At the start H. P. Mueller with an Auto-Union succeeded in getting off before Lang. He went into the lead with Lang snapping at his heels. Nuvolari in his Auto-Union was third, I was fourth. On the third lap I overtook Nuvolari, then I was behind Lang. We were driving wheel to wheel behind Mueller. Lang tried to pass but couldn't make it. That way we drove for eight laps. By and by we became annoyed. Lang waved at me, making a sign for me to try to pass. He let me go by and I decided to see whether it would work better by force than by polite waving of the arm. However, Mueller was so busy with his car that he neither heard nor saw anything.

In the hairpin turn of La Source, I decided, That's where I'll get him! Lang, behind me, waited in order to pass Mueller together with me. The La Source turn was too slippery. As I tried to by-pass the Auto-Union car in a wide curve, I slipped off the road.

Lang had meanwhile let Seaman get past him. Seaman was luckier than we because in the same lap—the ninth—Mueller drove up to the pits and Seaman had a free track ahead. He drove fast and sure in the rain. When he pulled up for refilling during the eighteenth lap, Lang was ahead by one lap, then he too had to refill and Seaman was in front again. Now Seaman began to increase speed with every lap—Lang had fallen back to 27 seconds, 28 seconds, on the twenty-second lap. During the twenty-third, just before the hairpin turn of La Source, it happened. . . .

Seaman had hit the dangerous, tricky corner too fast; his wheels touched the loose earth at the border of the road, started to skid, and he smashed with dreadful impact back into a tree and then, sideways, into another. There the car halted on all four wheels. The crash had broken the fuel pipe and the gasoline poured out onto the red-hot exhaust pipe. Seconds later the car was aflame.

Perhaps Seaman tried to save himself—but, as we later learned, he had suffered a severe kidney injury and his right arm was broken. It may have been also that the shock had caused him to lose consciousness so that he had not seen the trembling air nor felt the ominous heat.

It took minutes for spectators from the La Source bend to come running up to him through the pouring rain. The car was enveloped in a sea of flames. Courageous men tried, in spite of the fire, to save Seaman, but the victim was imprisoned by the steering wheel and they did not know how to work the lever to release it. After incredible efforts they succeeded in freeing Seaman, severely burned but alive.

Dr. Glaeser had meanwhile reached the scene of the accident. He sat in the ambulance with Seaman on the way to the hospital in Spa. For many hours he worked on Seaman, removing the shreds of skin that had turned to charcoal. Thighs, arms, hands and face severely burned. We were still standing in the spare-parts pit waiting for news. We knew only that Seaman's car was aflame—nothing more. Erika, who had become Seaman's wife a few months earlier, was standing beside me. She was white and trembling with cold and dread. We all feared the worst.

After the race was over we went to the Spa hospital. Dr. Glaeser was still bandaging Seaman. A little later Erika was permitted to see her husband. Dick was a hero. In spite of excruciating pain he tried to talk naturally, almost gaily, with his young wife.

Shortly after midnight Seaman died, conscious to the last, in the arms of his wife.

Erika was beside herself with grief. We took her to the hotel, to her room which was close to ours. Baby wanted to stay with her, but Erika said she wanted to try to sleep. After a few hours we heard a shy knock at the door. It was Erika. My wife took the frail little figure into her arms, held her head to her shoulder, and let Erika cry herself to sleep.

The following day we stood around a long, narrow coffin. Could Dick Seaman really have found room in that? Neubauer was deeply moved. He posted himself before the coffin and spoke to Dick. I no longer remember his exact words. I only know that it was a speech that moved us all deeply. Our wives sobbed and all of us had moist eyes. Neubauer's eyes, too, were swimming.

"Dick," he said, "we shall never forget you. You were a fair sportsman and a good friend to all of us."

We flew to England, escorting Richard Beatty Seaman home for the last time. Thus once more that year we stood at the grave of a highly gifted, promising young racing driver.

23

The Grand Prix of France, in Reims, was a success for Auto-Union. The three of us, Lang, Brauchitsch and I, chased each other for so long that we all turned sour in the end.

In mid-July we reported for the big one—the Grand Prix of Germany. Masses of people crowded around the entire Nuerburgring—250,000 to 300,000 spectators at least. The weather looked unpromising and we remarked, with gallows humor, "It's clearing up for a cloudburst."

Up there in the Eifel Mountains the weather changes rapidly. As yet it wasn't raining, but the turns in the woods were still moist. Preparing the cars was made extremely difficult by the uncertain weather. Rain tires? Light tires? What kind of spark plugs?

It was going to be a hard race. The Reims victory had given the drivers of Auto-Union renewed confidence. Our practice times were very close.

At the start the placement was as follows:

Caracciola	Brauchitsch	Lang
Mercedes	Mercedes	Mercedes
Brendel		Mueller
Mercedes		Auto-Union
Pietsch	Stuck	Nuvolari
Maserati	Auto-Union	Auto-Union

Hasse   Meier
Auto-Union   Auto-Union
Sommer   Dreyfus   Villoresi
Alpha-Romeo   Delahaye   Maserati
Raph   Joa
Delahaye   Maserati
Mandirola   Mazaud
Maserati   Delahaye

Right at the beginning of the race it became clear that we'd chosen the wrong plugs. Lang had to go to the pits during the second lap; later Brauchitsch had to stop to change spark plugs, too.

I was making out a little better. During the sixth lap I got Nuvolari, who was fighting back like a lion. But when I pulled up for refilling in the ninth, I had to change spark plugs too and lost a lot of time.

Mueller was refilling at the same time and took off before me. Hasse, too, passed while they screwed in the new plugs. Lang and Brauchitsch had to give up and I remained the only one from our team still in the race. And it was a long way yet to the finish.

The rain was pouring down now. In the twelfth lap I got Hasse and Mueller and worked to get some distance between myself and them because I knew I would have to pull up for refilling once again. By the fifteenth lap I was thirty-nine seconds ahead, then forty-four. I saw Neubauer's flag—it meant stop next time around. I drove precisely up to the flag in front of the pits. The mechanics put in sixty liters within seventeen seconds. Not a word was spoken. It was very quiet at the pit, everyone was tensed to the utmost. The eyes of the spectators were looking for Mueller. Would I get off before he passed me?

Finished and—off! My heart was dancing; I heard the high, singing, metallic sound of my car and I was driving on my beloved Nuerburgring, the fastest record lap to victory—my sixth victory in the German Grand Prix.

"The Old Master's Most Masterful Race" said the newspaper headlines. I was only thirty-eight years old and already they were calling me Old Master.

In August we met again in Bern. The clouds on the political horizon were gathering darkly. We did not want to believe in a coming war. It was impossible to think that we should be made to hate each other from one day to the next—we who were united here with many nations in fair and sporting competition.

It was a fast, hot race on a beautiful course. Lang was winner; I was second with four seconds behind my teammate.

In August, on the 25th, Louis Chiron was forty years old. He was in Villa d'Este, near Como, and asked us to come down with Brauchitsch to celebrate his birthday. We remained together for quite a while. It seemed as if the war might break out any day and we had so many things to tell each other. Before we parted we promised Chiron that we would phone him at once if we learned of such a catastrophe before he did, so that he could come to Lugano and escape being interned as a French Monacan by the Axis Italians.

Brauchitsch was ordered by Neubauer to come to the race in Belgrade. He left us with a heavy heart and gave us his luggage for safekeeping.

"Good-by, dear old Bear, good-by dear, sweet Baby!"

"Good-by, or rather—come back soon," I said.

September first was the fateful day. Now night was falling over Europe. I called Chiron in Villa d'Este and in the afternoon he was with us. On the morning of September 2 the word came: "War!"

We escorted Chiron to the station—he had to report for duty in Monte Carlo right away.

"*Adieu*, Louis, *au revoir, petit* Louis!"

"*Au revoir, grandfrère, et* Baby *chérie....*"

We returned to the empty house.

When evening came we looked for the little monkey, Anatol. All day long he had whistled to us from the tops of the highest trees. We could not see him in the thick foliage, but Anatol with his unbelievably sharp little eyes always saw us from far away.

His leather sleeping bag hung from the window shade. I looked inside and found to my astonishment that Anatol had already retired for the night. I reached into the bag, whereupon Anatol bit me. I called Baby, "Hey, Anatol bit me!"

Baby came, took the little monkey in her arms, and we saw that Anatol's thigh was injured. For ten days we nursed him, with no idea as to what had caused his injury. His favorite resting place during that time was on the top of my head. He'd clutch my hair and let his injured leg dangle. One night, he died in my wife's hands and then we found the hole and bullet. Anatol had been shot. His shrill whistling must have aroused the attention of some bloodthirsty hunter. Poor little Anatol. He had given us so much pleasure.

I remember an incident with him in Paris. It was summer and quite hot. Because of Anatol we left the window open a mere slot.

Toward nine in the morning we were awakened by someone knocking excitedly at our door. The page called:

"Monsieur, madame, your monkey is next door and the lady is afraid."

Baby quickly threw on a robe and hurried into our neighbor's room. Anatol, scared to death, was crouching way up on a curtain rod. She had to climb a ladder to get him down. Then the neighbor told her the story:

"Madame," she said, "I was awakened by somebody scratching in my hair and when I sat up I saw a monkey. I called out, 'Ernest come quickly! Here is a monkey looking for lice in my hair!' Ernest was in the bathtub and he called back, 'Go back to sleep, you're still drunk from last night!' "

Poor little Anatol. We buried him in our garden.

The sixteenth-century prophecies of the Maria Laach in the Eifel were being fulfilled:

"There will be a century of great wars which in intervals of decades will become ever greater and mightier and bloodier and more disastrous. After a dreadful war there will soon be another great war that will far surpass the first, in which Germania will be almost totally destroyed and crushed as by an avalanche of stone. Everything will be crushed and leveled, and this will come from east and west and north and south, tearing down all walls that have been built to withstand the avalanche . . . and fire will descend from the sky and poisonous clouds will sink down, destroying the people. Enormous dragons with heavy armor will spew out their poisonous breath and bring death and destruction wherever they may be. And great locusts will fly through the air and their excrements will be poison and food for Death, who will harvest them as never before."

A nightmare of dread.

24

The man I had seen for the first time in 1931 had become commander of the German armed forces—ruler over a Germany whose borders had been extended by force of arms. He wielded the power of life and death over a great nation.

This I had not thought conceivable and therefore I did not at that time consider my meeting him important.

A short while after my victory in the Mille Miglia race in Italy, in 1931, Dr. Kissel had called me to the plant. He told me that Herr Hitler, the leader of the National Socialist party, had ordered a convertible 7-liter Mercedes car. Hitler wanted a number of special things, such as a glove compartment shaped so that a revolver could conveniently be kept in it. Because of these special wishes the delivery date had not been kept and the important customer was annoyed. Dr. Kissel feared that he would not take delivery of the car.

Therefore, Dr. Kissel said, I was to take my newly won fame and go to Munich in order to present the car to Hitler personally and demonstrate it. Werlin, the Mercedes dealer in Munich, would accompany me and introduce me.

I went to Munich and while they washed the car, Werlin accompanied me to the "Brown House." At the entrance steps we were met by a tall, slim young man with wavy hair. It was Rudolf Hess. He asked us to wait, and after a short time led us into a large room. In one corner of that room was a desk and behind it sat Herr Hitler. He got up and came toward us: a rather stocky man with a trimmed mustache and straight black hair that fell over his forehead. He congratulated me on my great success in Italy. For the first time a German, in a Mercedes, a foreigner in Italy, had won the difficult 1600-kilometer race through that country!

His speech was clipped, tinged with Austrian-Bavarian accent. I thanked him for the congratulations and was searching for words to explain the purpose of my visit. But Hitler didn't even let me begin; Italy seemed to be a matter of burning interest to him. He wanted to know what living conditions were like there, whether the people were happy and how they felt about Mussolini. I answered the questions as well as I could. After all, I had seen Italy only at 100-kilometer speed! Time and again I opened my mouth to tell him that the automobile was ready now, that his special demands had caused the delay in delivery, but—he didn't give me a chance.

Still talking, Hitler offered to show us the Brown House. He led us into an enormous conference room, about 100 meters long—the so-called Senator's Hall. The rows of seats were raised as in a movie house and the chairs were covered with expensive, soft red leather. There was no stage; just a speaking platform. Then he showed us the basement where huge steel safes had been built into the walls. As we came in, a gentleman with a similar little mustache got up. He was, as I heard later, the Treasury chief, Schwarz. The safes contained the registry bearing the numbers and names of party members, their special identity and character, data, their relatives, whether they had served in the war and of what rank and capacity, plus the date of their entry into the party.

"Give me a membership card," said Hitler. "Say, number 1866."

Schwarz pulled out the card with this number. On it were a

person's name, professsion, marital status, number of children, date of entry into the party, and so on.

"Now then," said Herr Hitler, "give me the name card of this man."

Schwarz pulled a card from another safe, and on that one was the party number and the same information as on the previous card. In other words, double-entry bookkeeping, but with people instead of figures.

"My Fuehrer," said Schwarz, "I wish to report that today the five hundred thousandth member has been entered!"

Well, I thought, what do you know—quite a lot of people in this party. It was all very interesting, to be sure, but I felt that the moment had come to discharge my task.

"Herr Hitler," I said, "the big Mercedes you ordered is now ready. I've come to demonstrate it for you. It turned out to be a very beautiful car and I'm sure you will like it. May I bring it here?"

Hitler thought a moment.

"No," he said. "I'd prefer to look at it at the Mercedes garage. Expect me there in half an hour."

We went to the garage and Herr Hitler appeared punctually, accompanied by three men including his driver, Schreck.

While Werlin was explaining the details of the automobile, emphasizing how carefully the special demands had been carried out, Schreck took me aside.

"Herr Caracciola," he said, "under no circumstances must you drive faster than 30 kilometers an hour. The risk of accident must be reduced to a minimum. The enemies of our party would promptly use an accident for purposes of counterpropaganda."

The men got into the car and I took off, driving very slowly. I felt as if I could walk beside the car. I drove through the town and its environs, never faster than 30 kilometers. The test ride completely satisfied the customer. When I headed back for the garage, Hitler said:

"Herr Caracciola, I have a request. I'd like my niece to see this car. Would you take her around the block just once?"

I drove to the address he gave me. Hitler went into the house and came back with a young, golden-haired girl. She was so pretty that it took my breath away. Too bad I could take her around the block only once.

When we stopped in front of her house again she ran over to her uncle and exclaimed enthusiastically:

"Uncle, oh, Uncle, it's a magnificent car!"

The uncle beamed. As we drove off she waved for a long time.

In the garage I properly handed over the car and called Dr. Kissel to report that everything had worked out fine.

On the way back to Stuttgart I recalled the words of Treasurer Schwarz—the five hundred thousandth member. . . .

I could not imagine that this man would have the requirements for taking over the government some day. He had made no impression on me as a personality. Perhaps if he'd had the head of a Caesar, like Mussolini, possibly I'd have said, without a second thought:

"Herr Hitler, let me be number five hundred thousand and one." However, I hadn't, and Herr Hitler didn't seem to hold it against me. In later years, after he had taken over the government, I saw him several times when the racing cars drove up at the Chancellery prior to the opening of the Automobile Show in Berlin. He never forgot to inquire about my injured leg and always congratulated me on my victories.

In 1937 I had won the Grand Prix of Greater Germany and with it the coveted Adolf Hitler prize. It was a great, heavy bronze trophy—head with windblown hair and lightning darting at each side of it. I suppose it represented a god of speed or of the wind. The trophy was given to me after the race, at the Nuerburgring. Bernd Rosemeyer stood next to me. He was chewing on his cigarette and spitting out flecks of tobacco. Never before had I seen him so disappointed and dejected.

Brauchitsch was second.

The following morning he and I were asked to come to Hitler in Bayreuth. His private plane picked us up. In the morning there was a reception which Propaganda Minister Goebbels attended.

We were just standing around discussing the race. After half an hour we were still standing around. I could hear the clatter of dishes in the room next door. I felt hungry suddenly because we had breakfasted very early and then only very hastily.

"Manfred," I said, "I think we better go now. The Fuehrer will want to eat lunch, too."

And so we went.

Manfred told this story everywhere, to everyone's amusement. He kept saying that I should have been a diplomat.

We ate lunch in Bayreuth with Hitler's pilot, Bauer.

"Herr Caracciola," he said, "I must ask you something."

"Go ahead," I said.

"Some people in the Fuehrer's circle claim you have taken on Swiss citizenship. Is that true?"

I reached into my pocket and handed him my passport.

"Well," said Bauer. "Isn't that something! I'll clear that up at the next opportunity. I'll tell them that you're still a German."

"Now," I said, "I must ask *you* something."

"Yes?"

"Do you suppose you could fly us to Stuttgart?"

Mr. Bauer arranged the return flight and that evening we were back in Stuttgart.

The following day the firm threw a victory party. Dr. Kissel presented me with a diamond medallion with a sapphire Mercedes star. Each year the firm gave the victor one of these precious medallions. Each year they were different—diamonds with rubies, sapphires, or emeralds.

Only two years had passed since the reception in Bayreuth. And now under Hitler's rule war had broken out. All plans for the future had come to nothing. On both sides of the fighting fronts I had faithful friends.

Manfred von Brauchitsch had been ordered to attend the Belgrade race and then, with Neubauer, returned to Germany. We set about taking care of his possessions. Baby wrapped the woolens in newspapers, put in camphor balls, stuffed the shoes with tissue paper, bundled up the fragrant love letters, and then I helped her carry the bags up into the attic.

Within the first few days after the outbreak of the war, they began distributing gasoline coupons in Switzerland and soon everything except vegetables, fruit, poultry and fish was rationed. Each month you got a bar of chocolate on coupons.

Gradually the use of automobiles ceased altogether. Since I couldn't stand or walk for any length of time I sat incarcerated in my home as in a fortress. The pains in my hip, in my leg, were getting worse and worse. Perhaps I had too much time to think about them. Perhaps I should have that bone X-rayed again. We went to Bologna, to Professor Putti. He made me walk around for him a bit.

"*Lei un fenomeno,*" he said. "You are a phenomenon. With that leg you're still driving races? *Fantastico!*"

"Let's operate," said the first assistant, Scaglietti.

"Let's operate," said Professor Putti. "It's still time. That pseudoarthrosis will grow worse. You'll have more pains and the success of an operation will become more and more doubtful. Now we'd take out that piece of resorbed bone and put the head of the femur joint into the space of the removed fragment. You'll be a bit less mobile, but you'll be able to stand firmly. The difference in the length of the two legs won't be too noticeable because you won't sink in like that. Here, look at the X-rays of some successful operations which I've performed, almost exclusively on older persons. You'd have to stay with us three to four months before you can start walking again."

Three to four months—again in an iron bedstead in one of those convent-like hospital rooms and then learning to walk again, first in a wheel chair, then on crutches, and if the operation didn't succeed . . . I felt sick at the thought.

"Professor," I said, "I can't decide this so quickly. I've got to think it over carefully before I let you cut me up."

Professor Putti laughed, his dark eyes glowing.

"I understand, Signor Caracciola, I understand very well. It's a weighty decision. Come back or don't come back; do what you feel you want to do. You'll remain my *carissimo fenomeno*."

With rapid steps he hurried down the endlessly long corridor, his white coat fluttering behind him, his white hair shining in the fading sunlight. I gazed after him until he disappeared from sight. I never saw him again. He has since gone to the Valhalla of great surgeons, the helpers of mankind.

When I arrived in the dark hotel room with the polished stone floor, I lay down on the bed. I felt unspeakably worn out, physically and mentally. Baby sat down opposite me. For a long time we were silent, each thinking his own thoughts, each searching for a solution.

"You know, Rudi darling," she said then, "of course there are no pictures of operations that didn't succeed. There aren't going to be any races for a long time. Perhaps never again. Now you can rest a lot more and for everyday use the old bone is plenty good enough. An operation is a tricky thing. You know what you've got, but you never know what you'll get!"

I felt exactly the way she did, but I was glad that she spoke the deciding, liberating words. Suddenly I was enormously hungry.

"Come on, little one," I said. "Now we're going out to dinner. To Papagallo's for *Tagliatelle verde alla Bolognese*, and tomorrow we're going home!"

The Swiss government issued a proclamation requesting every citizen to plant vegetables on every inch of soil. My carefully nursed lawn was dug up to plant potatoes, and in the flower garden we put in corn, tomatoes, string beans, lettuce and leeks. The ground should be terraced about three feet, I decided, so that my back wouldn't hurt so much. I could barely bend over, and so it was Baby who squatted on the ground, heaping up the earth around the corn stalks and pulling weeds. Now I learned all about insect pests and what a hailstorm could do to a crop.

Twice a year the hail destroyed our crop. It came down from the growling sky like pigeons' eggs. After the storm everything lay torn and broken on the ground. Never again, I thought; never again a garden, never again this labor. But next day we started again from scratch. I never realized what fun it was to see the things growing that you yourself have planted.

In a coop we kept some Sussex chickens that gave me an hour's work each day preparing their feed. The corn was rationed, a kilo every three months for three chickens. Rationing permitted one and a half chicken per person. So I had to mash up chestnuts, bread crusts, cabbage leaves and greens to feed the little creatures. Time was entirely filled with these everyday tasks. We lived, figuratively speaking, behind high walls.

Most of my money was in Germany because after 1933 no money could be transferred abroad without special permission. And those permissions were very hard to get. I had wanted to give my wife a fur coat for our wedding in 1937 but the foreign exchange authorities refused to release the money for it.

When war broke out, Dr. Kissel, director general of the Daimler-Benz Company arranged for me to get a pension that would enable me to live in Switzerland and to remain with Mercedes. Dr. Kissel informed me of this in the following words:

"In view of the enormous services rendered us with the skill and courage of your driving throughout all the years in which you took part in racing and other sports events for our firm, we are allocating on your behalf the salary of a director. Let us take this opportunity to thank you once again with all our heart for the victories you've won for us. At the same time we wish to express our gratitude to your wife for the devoted co-operation she has so generously given us on every occassion."

Two years went by. The leg, now well rested, began to behave a lot better. I began to ask myself what the future held in store for me. I wanted to drive races as soon as the hostilities were over. How dreadful the war would be was not to be fore-seen early in 1941. I had no car. And a racing car would have meant more to me than anything else.

In 1941 I went to Stuttgart to discuss my plans and my wishes with Dr. Kissel. I had a notion of taking over a little 1500-cc. Tripolis racing car which I would keep in top shape in my garage until the day when there would be races again. Dr. Kissel said he would think it over, and the next day he called me in to his office again.

"My dear Caracciola," he said, "nowhere would the car be in better hands than with you. I'd say both cars, in fact, since only one of them is in working shape. You'd have to use the other as a sort of spare-parts supply depot, because except for a few minor parts we have no spare parts for these cars. I'd like to give you these cars but they cannot be taken out of Germany. It would be considered illegal export of property. As soon as the transfer of the cars can be done officially, I'll have them brought over to you. You know that anything in writing about this would be considered a violation of the foreign exchange laws under present conditions."

I left Dr. Kissel, my beloved, respected fatherly friend who since 1927 had been a stern but just boss—little knowing that his handclasp was, for me, his final farewell.

The difficulties started in 1942. In April my pension was blocked as a result of an order by the NSKK (the National Socialist Automobile Corps). I had not obeyed the order calling me back to Germany. Since my injuries had left me unfit for army duty, I was supposed to devote myself to troop entertainment. This I couldn't do. I could not find it in myself to cheer up young men so that they would believe in a victory I myself could not believe in.

Dr. Kissel died suddenly in July—a heart attack—while spending a weekend in Ueberlingen on Lake Constance. I was deeply shocked and made immediate preparations to go to Stuttgart for the funeral. A telephone call to Stuttgart prevented me from carrying out my plans. I was told that the cool weather might be bad for my health and that it would be definitely better if I stayed home.

I hung up and thought over what had been said. . . . So that's what was meant! So it had come to that. The threatening finger of the NSKK was pointing at me personally.

A few weeks later, Huehnlein, the head of the NSKK, died. He had been rather conciliatory on my behalf—a bumbling, good-natured fellow who had honestly believed in his national-socialistic ideal, and who got neither riches nor advantages from his position.

25

Slowly, hopelessly, the gruesome years crept by, bringing misery and destruction and finally ending in a peace that was no peace. The few letters that reached us were covered all over with blue stripes and many passages had been rendered illegible by the censor's pen.

Except for the visit of an occasional friend we lived entirely by ourselves. Peter de Paolo, the former American racing champion who had won the greatest victory of his career in the 500-mile Indianapolis race in 1925, visited me. He was a colonel in the American Air Force, stationed in Zurich to take care of the Flying Fortresses that had landed in Switzerland.

He came frequently to Lugano for the weekend and of course we talked about automobile racing. I told him that I still had hopes of getting my little Mercedes silver arrows into my hands.

Dr. Kissel's closest associate, Dr. Wilhelm Haspel, had taken his place. Dr. Haspel sometimes came to Switzerland on business, and in 1943 I went to Zurich to see him there. At first I didn't know how to go about asking him about "my" cars. I couldn't do it in a public restaurant and the hotel room might be wired. Haspel himself suggested, after dinner, that we go for a little walk. We went down the Bahnhofstrasse, and, while looking at the brightly lit shop windows, we talked.

"Dr. Kissel told me at the time in strictest confidence that you were to get the Tripolis cars as soon as a transfer was possible," he said. "For the time being this is absolutely out of the question. To use a truck for purposes other than military is a crime for which one can be shot. So I can't do anything right now except assure you that when the time comes I shall do everything to keep the promise of my predecessor. The cars are safe; they're walled in in an absolutely bombproof air-raid shelter near Dresden. Only a few of our most reliable people know where they are."

Early in 1945, a few months before the final collapse of Germany, Peter de Paolo called me.

"Rudi," he said. "Your little Mercedes babies are in Zurich!"

"Impossible!" I said.

"I saw them," Peter said jubilantly. "And tomorrow you'll see a picture of them crossing the border, in the *Automobil Revue*."

Peter was mistaken, I was absolutely sure. Even so we took the next train to Zurich and went to the Mercedes-Benz AG garage.

"Where are the cars?" I asked Muff, the director.

Muff looked at me with his mouth open. "How do you know that the cars have arrived?"

"The Americans told me," I said. "And tomorrow the news is going to be in the *Automobil Revue*."

The director began to recover from his astonishment. He led us into a large repair shop in the basement and there they were, the glorious little cars. One could see that they had endured a difficult, dangerous trip. In the chaos, the disorganization of the German collapse, a few faithful Mercedes people had managed to get up a truck. The cars were literally chopped out of their hideout (they had been cemented in), put on the truck, and then were driven, avoiding the major highways, through ruins and burning villages all the way to the Swiss border. The men unloaded them, turned them over to customs, and went away.

The customs men recognized the cars and since there were no

papers or documents accompanying them, they called Mercedes-Benz AG in Zurich, the firm that had imported Mercedes cars before the war. The Zurich firm sent people to the border, a director coming along in person; the duties were paid and the cars brought to Zurich.

I had asked several times whether there wasn't any news about the cars, but since all communications had been broken, and no instructions arrived with the cars, the Zurich firm had felt entitled to take them over.

I kept walking around and around the cars. Dr. Kissel had been right—one car was not complete and had furthermore been damaged in transport.

Now the little silver arrows would soon come home with me, I thought. I had not taken into consideration the import laws of the Swiss authorities and the Allied Commission that was in charge of German property. No sooner had the cars passed over the threshold of the Mercedes garage than they were requisitioned as German property.

Baby and I returned to Lugano with heavy hearts. Life seemed empty indeed. It was as if I'd lifted a magnificent treasure from the bottom of the sea only to see it drop down and out of reach again.

On March 14, 1946 I received a telegram from Pop Meyers, the vice president of the Indianapolis speedway. He invited me, my wife, a mechanic, and the little Mercedes car to come to Indianapolis to take part in the race of May 30, the 500-mile Indianapolis race.

"That's impossible," I said.

"Impossible? Well, let's see about *that!*" said my wife.

There followed a period of improbabilities, miracles and petty details. But above all that happened, shone the people's love of sports, sports that united countries, sports wherein nothing counted except performance and achievement. It seemed as if every place I had to go for permission took its own special delight in the project. Closed doors opened, willing hands reached out and helped, until the great plan *almost* became reality. Two fateful words destroyed all our hopes and indirectly caused the worst calamity of my life. The words were: "Decidedly no. . . ."

Above all, I had to obtain an alien identity card from the Bern authorities because my passport had become invalid and there was not as yet an authority in charge of passport renewals. I submitted an application to the Swiss property control office, requesting them to release one of the two requisitioned cars for participation in the Indianapolis race.

Eventually the strict rules were relaxed:

"Release of one car for repair and participation in the 500-mile race. Two months' leave from the requisition."

However, the property control office was not the final authority. We had to get the permission of the political department in Bern and of the Inter-Allied Commission. I had to get an American visa and it was not easy for a German to obtain one.

Cables flew back and forth between Zurich and Washington, up to a hundred and forty-two words per cable. I also had to find a way to bring my faithful mechanic, Walz, to Zurich and I had to get the blueprints of the motor and spare parts if those were still available.

So I had to drive to Stuttgart. And there were no visas for entering Germany. Since I couldn't go there officially I had to do it unofficially. . . .

Baby remembered a young French lieutenant of the occupation army whom I'd met a few months earlier. At that time he'd invited me to visit him some time. I'd need neither passport nor visa, he had told me; he'd meet me at the border.

"Let's visit him," she said. "Once we're over the border we'll go on from there somehow."

No sooner said than done. We packed food and cigarettes

and took along two large cans of gasoline and several wrist watches.

On March 24 we took off. The lieutenant was waiting for us at the border. We followed him to the little villa where he lived. A nice little house—requisitioned of course.

Lunch was being served and as the maid brought in the soup she nearly dropped the tureen.

"Jesus, it's Caratchola!" she exclaimed.

"How do you know me?"

"Before the war I had seen you so often in the newspaper and at the Schauinsland race," she said. "I recognized you right off. Oh, wait till I tell my husband—won't he be happy to hear that I seen you!"

Our host then asked whether we would spend the night with him—he'd be glad to make up the beds in the guest rooms. Now I had to be frank. I had to tell him the true reason for my visit. And I told him that I simply had to get to Stuttgart and hoped that he could give me a *laisser-passer* for the French zone so that I could then sneak into Stuttgart from Tuebingen.

The lieutenant was afire with enthusiasm when he heard my plans, but he was not entitled to issue a *laisser passer*.

"Wait, Monsieur Caracciola. I'll go and talk to our commandant. He's a good man, perhaps he can help you."

He left. Baby and I sat waiting for the verdict that would decide success or failure of our plan. The lieutenant came back soon.

"The commandant asked to see you. He'd like to talk to you, to meet you."

The commandant received us and I told him about the invitation to come to America, and about the almost insurmountable difficulties. He listened in silence. He understood my French and he understood German, too.

"Monsieur Caracciola," he said, "in the library of this house I found your book and a short while ago I read it. Let me tell you that I am sincerely happy to make your acquaintance. I'll be glad to help you and to do what I can for you. I can give you a *laisser-passer* for the French zone, but that isn't valid for the American zone. Your mechanic won't get an exit permit from the American zone, but if you should manage to have him transferred to the French zone, tell him to report to me at once. I'll escort him into Switzerland personally. The only prerequisite for his entry into Switzerland is that an entry permit is ready for him at the border. I wish you all the best of luck, Monsieur. If, as a German, you should succeed in racing with a German car in America, that would be the first sign of friendship between nations brought about through their common love of sports. *Bonne chance*, Monsieur."

I was deeply moved. To hear such words from a French officer was most heart-warming.

"*Mon Commandant*," I said, "how is it possible that you can have such a generous attitude so soon after this war?"

"*Monsieur*," he replied, "we Frenchmen are fated by geography to have a common border with the Germans. The sooner we find a way to true peace, the better it will be for all of us."

We got a *laisser-passer* for the French zone on which was printed: "With this permit you may not enter the American zone."

Baby laughed. "If they won't let us enter with this permit, we will simply throw it out the window when we reach the border!"

I had met a Swiss who resided in Stuttgart and had invited us to stay with him if I "made it."

There was no sign of a zonal border, except for some American soldiers sitting at the side of the road around a campfire. One of them took a notion to ask us for identification. Those were unpleasant moments. I solemnly handed him the car's document which was covered with seals and stamps. That seemed to satisfy him and he let us drive on. Only later did I learn that, had he examined the car, I would surely have been thrown in jail. We had cans of gasoline and American cigarettes —it was strictly contraband.

It was beginning to get dark. I drove faster. A jeep appeared. How fast were those jeeps anyhow? Baby glanced back.

"Listen," she said, "those little things are really fast. He's really sticking to us. And how that guy drives! He looks really grim. Why don't you step on it—let's see how fast they can really go."

The speedometer showed 120 (75 miles an hour). I had to slow down behind a truck and the jeep caught up with me and came alongside and then cut in front of me, forcing me to stop.

The man got out. He had the letters MP on his helmet and his magnificent German shepherd also had a yellow MP on his blue coat. I've rarely ever seen such rage as this man displayed.

"You," he roared, "you—what do you think you're doing? Haven't you ever heard about speed limits? Your papers!"

"But, mister," said Baby, "didn't you see how I kept turning around to look at you. We were so impressed with the performance of your jeep, we wanted to know how fast such a jeep can go."

"My jeep's none of your business," he growled, still leafing through my papers, which again served our purpose.

"Where are you going?" he demanded.

"To Switzerland, to Lugano," I said.

"Wherever you're going, you'll never get there *this* way. You'd land in the cemetery first."

I nodded agreeably and drove very slowly until the next bend. You never stop learning. Now I knew that the jeeps were frequently occupied by military police and I had also learned how fast they were. My curiosity was satisfied.

The sight of Stuttgart was heart-rending. No newspaper report could convey what the eyes beheld. I kept asking myself where the people I saw lived—the houses were almost all bombed out or damaged.

The next morning I drove to Untertuerkheim, to the factory.

I found a field of rubble there. They were clearing the rubble away; everybody was shoveling and carrying off debris. All the employees of the firm were helping, voluntarily and without pay, regardless of rank or position. "Our" factory had to be rebuilt, "our" star had to shine again.

Dr. Wilhelm Haspel was no longer with the firm. As a former big industrialist he was now having an especially hard time. While I was there he was in the hospital, where I visited him and told him about the invitation to Indianapolis.

He told me to go and see the two acting directors of the firm, Dr. Otto Hoppe and Dr. Kaufmann, both of whom then proceeded to help me.

I got permission to look around the selected junk from the rubble for parts and tires, for a feed pipe and wheels. I found quite a bit I could use very well.

They also arranged for Walz and another specialist to be transferred into the French zone after our efforts to get an exit permit from the American zone had become hopeless.

On April 5 Walz arrived in Zurich. The French commandant had kept his word and Baby had obtained entry permits for Walz and the second mechanic.

The preparation of the car was not easy, although we had blueprints of the motor. Among other things we did not have Duroflex tubes, which were unobtainable. An American friend from the embassy gave me some tubes from his airplane. The special fuel had to be prepared and a reserve oil container had to be built on the side of the car because Indianapolis doesn't permit oil refills during the race.

When the car was ready I wanted to drive it at least for a short stretch to see if everything was indeed perfect. I went to the police to ask if they would permit me to drive a short lap at full speed. The Zurich police being very sports-minded, one morning, at five, they closed off a long straight street for me to do some trial runs. The car ran like a precision watch and reached a high speed right off. I cannot describe how happy we were. The Swiss mechanic, Friedly, my dear Walz, and I—we just looked at one another. There are moments in life which one never forgets.

Unfortunately I would not be able to take Walz along to America. As a German residing in Germany, he couldn't get an exit visa to go to the United States. So it was Friedly, of Bern, who was to go along in order to take care of the car over there. Meanwhile Baby was getting the visas: a transit visa for France; an English transit visa for Newfoundland; all these were actually almost impossible for a German to obtain with an alien registration card in Switzerland. A re-entry permit for Switzerland—and we already had the U.S. entry permit.

Finally we had everything. The car, too, was ready and I had to give some thought to packing it. I'd had a large wooden crate made and the car and my tools were stashed away in it. Then we had to find a truck that would hold the crate, and have all the necessary papers for driving to France and putting the car aboard a ship in a French port.

When that was done, a dockworkers' strike broke out in France and the driver now had to get papers to go to Belgium. On April 17 I learned that England had not yet granted permission for the temporary "exit" of the car from Switzerland. We turned to people we thought could help us, in Bern and in London. On April 18 the British trade attaché in Bern told us he was not the proper authority and we should approach the Foreign Office directly.

We asked a friend in London to explain the case to the Foreign Office and to ask them to issue us permission for the temporary export of the car from Switzerland to the United States. This was done and we waited hopefully. On April 24 I had the crate with the car loaded on the truck. There was no more time to be lost if we still wanted to catch the boat. It was the last boat we could take because the race was on May 30. And I had yet to practice and take the obligatory practice laps and the driver's test on the course.

Peter de Paolo and the organizers of the 500-mile race were following this entire procedure with suspense. Long cables were exchanged back and forth. Finally, when it became hopeless to try and reach the ship, I got a cable from de Paolo. He told me that they had contacted General Doolittle and that the car would be flown to the States on a transport plane when—and if—I got permission from London to take the car out of Switzerland.

Toward evening that day came the bad news: The Foreign Office refused permission.

Until April 30 I tried in vain to get them to reverse their decision. No success.

I went back to Lugano. Baby received me, looking pale and tired. We could not seem to grasp the fact that all our efforts, all our work, all this trouble and expense should have been entirely in vain.

"Baby, listen," I said. "I've had an idea. We'll go to Indianapolis anyhow. It'll be helpful next year if I get to know the course now, if I see the race and the way things are done."

And that's what we did. We flew to America. A beautiful flight with TWA from Zurich via Paris, Shannon, Newfoundland to New York.

At the airport we were met by René Dreyfus, the well-known French racing champion. He escorted us to the hotel and then to his charming and excellent restaurant, Le Gourmet. We stayed in New York only briefly because I wanted to see as much as possible of the practice in Indianapolis.

In an overcrowded train we journeyed to Indianapolis. We took a sleeping compartment. The following morning when we went into the dining car for breakfast we didn't believe our eyes: there they sat: Achille Varzi, Gigi Villoresi, the well-known sports writer Filippini; Mazuchelli, the Ferrari man; the entire Italian team that was to participate in the Indianapolis race. What a happy, noisy reunion! We spoke Italian, German—nobody paid any attention. Nobody cared what language we spoke. We had not seen each other since the outbreak of the war.

Pop Meyers awaited us in Indianapolis, with Wilbur Shaw, the triple winner of the Indianapolis race and president of the speedway; Dolly Dallenbach, the secretary who was the heart and soul of the speedway office; and Peter de Paolo. All that was needed was a band and flowers.

I met the new owner of the autodrome, Mr. Anton Hulman, Jr., a couple of days after we arrived. He gave me a warm handshake.

"I've longed for this day, Rudi," he said. "I've heard so much about you and read so much about you that I wanted to meet you. I'm sorry you had to come without your little Mercedes. I couldn't have thought of anything more wonderful than for you to drive on my course in that masterpiece of the German automobile industry. I must tell you that my grandfather, who founded the firm of Hulman & Co., emigrated from Germany in the middle of the last century. He came from Lingen."

Tony made me feel as if I'd known him all my life. From the day of our meeting we were close friends.

A room had been reserved for us at the Marott Hotel. Right after my arrival at the hotel, the clerk handed me a letter. In unusual block letters was the following message:

"Rudolph Caracciola:
I want to talk to you tomorrow morning before you leave the hotel. I'm staying in this hotel, too. It concerns a car of mine which you can drive.

Joe Thorne

At first I wasn't going to pay attention to the letter, but then I became intrigued by the idea of getting to know the Indianapolis course in an American racing car instead of merely driving through it in a limousine. So I went to see Joe Thorne the following morning. Thorne, a very well-to-do, odd, lean young man had a workshop in the infield of the autodrome. He had his own technical staff and mechanics working for him, and owned two remarkably fast racing cars that ran under the name "Thorne Engineering Special." One of them was a nonsupercharged 4½ liter, six-cylinder engine with a carburetor for each cylinder. This was the car I was to drive. Joe Thorne had meant to enter the race with that car, but couldn't because of a motorcycle accident in which he'd fractured his leg badly. Although he had to move around in a wheel chair, he first insisted on taking part anyhow, but the racing management refused him permsission to start for reasons of safety.

"Nobody is going to drive this car, Mr. Caracciola, unless it is you," Thorne said. "I'd not entrust this car to anyone else. Robson is driving my other car. That one is good too, but this one is faster."

In the afternoon we drove out to the course to have a look at the car. It looked rather tall. The driver's seat was suspended freely in the chassis and small shock absorbers controlled its motion. That way the driver was protected from jolts. The car had four-wheel brakes operated by a hand brake fastened outside the body of the car. Astonished, I asked the purpose of the arrangement. Thorne told me that this way the driver following you could see at once when the man ahead of him pulled the brake. Actually one hardly ever pulls the brake on a course.

Some vague hunch had caused me, before leaving Zurich, to go to the Mercedes garage and pick up my racing case in which I had my racing clothes, shoes and goggles. Now they would come in handy.

I changed clothes, got into the car and was about to leave the inner area for the track—but right away a supervisor stopped me.

"No, Rudi, you can't do that," he said. "First you've got to get a crash helmet, then you have to be examined by a doctor.

When everything is checked, you can take your driver's exam for this course and then you can take off."

Growling, I got out and went to the stands where the doctor had his office during practice. He examined me thoroughly, then asked my age.

"I'm forty-five," I said.

He examined my eyes—I had to read large and small letters from close up and from a distance. There was a tiny "y" and I didn't know what you called that in English.

"How do you call that funny little tripod letter?" I asked Dr. Smith.

"Never mind, never mind," he said, laughing. "You have eyes like an eagle! Your blood pressure is 110, your heart beats as calmly as an old truck engine. Wait till I tell the boys—forty-five years old and in such great shape!"

Now that I had the doctor's okay, where did I get a crash helmet?

Al Herrington, president of the AAA, got me a British tank crash helmet. It was very light with air vents, but solid. I put it on and it felt as if my head was in a bucket. Now at last I could get out on the course.

I felt my way around the car and studied the course and the corners very carefully. This oval square was surprising—each corner had to be approached differently. The corners were only slightly elevated, the back stretch was wide and beautiful. The front stretch, before the stands, on the other hand, was uneven and bumpy because it was paved with bricks. Formerly the entire course had been like that but eventually they had to cover the corners and at least one of the straightaways with asphalt. After a few laps I had the car in hand. The pickup power was tremendous and the car hugged the road splendidly.

I found the mica windshield too high and drove back to the pits to ask Thorne if we could not cut it down a bit. That was actually the only thing I found wrong with the car.

26

The following day I decided to take the driver's test. I had to drive ten laps at an average speed of 140 and 160 kilometers per hour and five more at over 160 kilometers per hour. These average speeds had to be kept rigidly.

It all went well. I liked the car; actually I might drive the qualification laps; that is, four laps at over 190 kilometers per hour.

I pulled up at the pits and had new tires put on, just to be safe. Meanwhile the report on my exam came in. They said I'd driven like clockwork. I smoked another cigarette, put on the crash helmet and got into the car.

Seth Klein, the starter and director of the racing program, came to the car.

"Now Rudi," he said, slapping me on the shoulder, "you understand—you're alone on the course now, to take the qualification laps. You do a few laps and, once you've warmed up, lift your hand when you pass the starting line and we clock you. Take four laps in succession. If you're not satisfied with your time you can break off—you're allowed three attempts to qualify."

I touched the crash helmet with two fingers.

"Okay, chief, I'll see what I can do. . . ."

The road was free. I drove out of the pits, turned a few laps to warm up the motor and roughen up the tires. Two, three more laps, I thought, and then I raised my hand. The car flew across the course—and that's the last thing I knew.

I didn't know anything for a long, long time. Actually I learned what had happened after several weeks, from what Baby told me later.

During my warm-up laps she was standing at the rail on the side of the stands, behind a strong, high mesh-wire fence that separated the spectators from the course. Suddenly she saw people running to the right back corner, and fire engines and an ambulance raced to the scene of the accident. And it was clear that there *was* an accident; and that it was I, was also certain, because there was nobody else on the course.

Baby crossed the course through the underpass and on the other side she found herself again blocked by a wire fence that separated the spare-parts depots and repair shops from the track. A man was sitting at a little table a few yards away from her.

"Hello, sir," she said. "I am Alice Caracciola. My husband must have had an accident, I must go to him. I must go with him in the ambulance to the hospital."

The man got up and came over to the fence.

"The ambulance is already gone, madam," he said. "But I'm going to get a car right away and we'll take you to the hospital."

Lou Meyers and another man brought her to the hospital, with the sirens of a police escort making way for them. When she arrived at the Methodist Hospital I was already in the emergency room on the ground floor, on an operating table. My face was purple and swollen. I was gasping. My coveralls were hanging in shreds from my arms and my back. After they'd cleaned me and the doctors determined that none of my limbs were broken, I was put in a bed with side guards.

By and by many people came to ask how I was. Until late in the night the anteroom was full of visitors. Joe Thorne, the mechanics, Mary and Tony Hulman, Wilbur Shaw and many others. They all hoped that I would regain consciousness and be able to explain what had happened.

Something had hit me on the temple and the guard of that part of the course had said that Caracciola's hands had suddenly dropped from the steering wheel and Caracciola himself had suddenly collapsed. The driverless car had then shot at top speed into the wooden barrier that enclosed the course on the back straightaway. The driver had been thrown out in a great arc and had hit the pavement with the back of his head. The car had turned over several times and had stopped just before the inert body of the driver.

Actually this accident, like most accidents, has never really been explained satisfactorily. The dead don't speak. And to those who are severely injured, nature mercifully robs the memory of the instant of terror. I don't think I know anybody who survived a near-fatal accident who was able to describe the seconds before or after.

Two days after my accident the 500-mile race took place. George Robson, on the Thorne Engineering Special, Joe Thorne's second car, won the race—a kind of justice to make up for the loss of the car I had driven. Robson did not enjoy the seventy thousand dollars long. A few months later he suffered a fatal accident.

After the race a man came to the hospital and asked to speak to me. Baby received him and let him see me through the open door, and then asked what he wanted. He showed an FBI badge.

"Madam," he said, "may I ask you to show me your passports or other travel documents?"

Baby had her passport and my alien registration card in her bag. She showed him these documents which were loaded with the many seals and visas we had needed for this trip. The FBI man carefully examined the alien registration card, which bore the American entry permit, valid for two months' stay in the States.

"Well, of course," he said. "It couldn't be otherwise. I thought so right away. Caracciola is too well known to come in without proper papers."

Baby was astonished. What did he mean?

"Madam," said he, "there has been a complaint against your husband. Somebody reported that he had entered the country with false documents and I was told to arrest him before the start of the race. I looked for him. Then I heard of the accident, so I came here. Let me tell you something. Perhaps you have skunks in Europe, but believe you me, we have them here too! I hope your husband will recover soon, madam, but make sure he stays as long as necessary for him to recover completely. You'd better apply for a three months' extension of your entry permit right now. I'll give you the address of the office you should write to—I'll personally recommend that your application be approved."

Then he left, his head bowed as if deep in thought, and walked with slow steps down the hall.

Baby was deeply shocked. With cruel clarity this anonymous denunciation had shown that there were among the drivers some who would not tolerate intruders.

Two weeks after the accident Wilbur Shaw brought back my goggles. I believe they were examined carefully, but I was never told the meaning of the deep holes in the unbreakable glass and steel frame of the goggles.

Since 1946, guards have been posted every fifty yards on the Indianapolis course, both during practice and the actual race.

When Tony Hulman came to the hospital in the evening, Baby told him about the visit from the FBI.

"Alice," he said, "if Rudi had been at the start and if the

FBI man had come to arrest him, I wouldn't have let the race start before Rudi's papers were looked at, which would have straightened everything out right away."

For five consecutive days and five nights Baby remained at my bedside, never taking her eyes off me. After forty-eight hours my breathing grew calmer, but my right side was paralyzed and my coma so deep that the doctors could not open my mouth.

One night, toward two in the morning, while the life-sustaining glucose ran into my veins, Baby decided to go to the hotel to change her bloodstained clothes. At the hospital people ordered a cab by giving their name and address. So she called a cab and gave her name.

"Oh, are you the wife of the injured racing driver?" said the voice on the telephone.

"Yes, I'm Mrs. Caracciola."

"I'll be there right away, madam."

The cab arrived. The driver, a huge man with sunburned face and light blue eyes got out to open the door for Baby. On the way to the hotel he said:

"That's terrible, madam, to come from so far away only to crash here. I hope with all my heart that your husband will soon recover. How is he?"

"He's still unconscious and the right side is paralyzed. More than that no one can tell."

"Please let me be at your disposal, madam. Call me any time of day or night, whenever you need me. Remember, McLean is my name. I'm with the Red Cab Company."

On the sixth night Baby was able to go to the hotel for a few hours and so she called McLean. He arrived at the hospital almost instantly.

"How is the boy?" he asked immediately.

"He's a little better," Baby told him. "Today, for the first time, he moved his right arm, and the doctors were able to open his mouth for the first time. Now we hope that he'll come to soon."

"I knew he'd be better today, madam."

"Why? How did you know that?"

"Madam," said McLean, "when it comes right down to it, one can help—only the Big Boss up there. When I left you last night I went home and went down on my knees and I prayed to God with all my heart to help your husband."

Until now Baby had been so brave. But at this she broke down and wept, and with the tears for the many disappointments and the dreadful accident were mingled tears of gratitude that I was alive and that a stranger in a foreign land had prayed for a man unknown to him.

From the sixth day on I was gradually able to move. The arm into which the glucose was dripping had to be tied on a board, and that had to be tied to the bed. My eyes, that had been turned up in my head, came down finally and wanted to see, but closed in shock before the strange surroundings. On the tenth day came words and brief recognition. I kept asking for Tony.

Then I talked from morning to night and the questions were always the same. Three nurses took turns, and after their eight-hour shift left the room exhausted. Only Baby saw it through—for her the day contained twenty-four hours.

Gradually I began to be aware of sighs, the desperate cries of the severely injured who were brought to this emergency wing from the street. Why was I here? I was healthy. Why was I here while another man screamed in pain? The one who screamed like that—why didn't they put him into this bed? I must get out, I must get away!

Hotel Marott. . . . Marott Hotel, Room 115, North Meridian. I bent the iron bars of the hospital bed as if they were made of wax. I kicked them with my feet until the whole bed looked a wreck. I had to be careful so that Baby wouldn't notice—she wouldn't let me get up. . . .

"What are you doing, Rudi darling?"

"Nothing, nothing," I said. I must speak only English so no one can know that I'm German. I'm imprisoned here. Those who scream there are being beaten day and night. Soon they'll beat me. I must get away.

"Tony, help. . . . Baby, where are you? You're never here."

"But I'm here, Rudilein, I'm always here."

"No, you always go away."

Baby brought me vanilla ice cream. Ice cream was great. Oh, how marvelous that ice cream tasted. I laughed with pleasure. But I had to get away from here.

Baby went to the hospital cafeteria for something to eat. The moment had come. I first pushed my feet between the foot and the side bars of the bed, then I bent the side bars down. It worked. I was standing.

I was so dizzy, I had to hold on the furniture, to the wall, until I reached the open door. I looked down the hall to left and right. If only no one came now. Out—into the hall—the open door to the right. . . . I could escape, there, in the driver's seat of the ambulance. The driver was standing alongside.

"Marott Hotel," I said. "Room 115."

"All right," he said. "In just a moment."

Before I could grasp what was going on they surrounded me. There she was, the bespectacled owl of a nurse; there that idiot who talked to me as if I were sick, and there was also a man with a policeman's cap. I defended myself with all my power, kicking, punching, there—another kick against the shin of that bespectacled owl. They overpowered me, put me to bed and tied me up.

Baby, having finished her coffee, walked back through the

foyer toward my room. There the hospital policeman sat in shirt sleeves, his cap pushed back on his head. The heat was unbearable.

"Hi, there, girl," he called to her, "you better watch out for your fellow there. He's up to no good—he raised hell around here."

Breathlessly Baby came running into the room. I behaved like a very nice little boy so she wouldn't notice anything.

"Rudi, what are you doing?"

"Nothing," I said innocently.

"If you keep this up they won't let me stay with you. Then you'll be all alone in a small, dark room."

The brain specialists, Dr. Hahn, Dr. Merrell, and the resident doctor ordered complete rest. They had not yet X-rayed my head because they did not want to raise me from the horizontal position. After my escapade, Baby talked to the doctors. She asked them to X-ray my head, and also she asked them to let her take me to the hotel.

"He wants to go to the Marott Hotel," she said. "He thinks he's a prisoner. He thinks those who scream are being beaten. He hears the crying and sobbing in the other rooms now and he doesn't understand what that is. He doesn't know that accident victims are dying here daily. He doesn't know that there are sometimes pools of blood in the hall."

They X-rayed me and the X-rays showed neither a fracture nor a crack in my skull. After a long conference the doctors gave me permission to leave the hospital. They told my wife:

"If you take the responsibility, you can take Rudi to the hotel."

The evening before my release Baby talked with me for a long time. She tried to make me understand that I'd had an accident on the Indianapolis race course. I had to laugh. I'd never been in Indianapolis! She then brought newspapers and pictures showing a man in a racing car. The man wore a crash helmet and looked exactly like me.

"Listen," I said. "You're a pretty bright girl usually. Don't you see this is a fake? Well done, though. These Americans are very ingenious. But *you* should know that *I*'ve never in my life worn such a thing as a crash helmet."

The next morning they dressed me and we drove to the hotel. The pretty nurses and the bespectacled owl waved to me:

"Good-by, Rudi, good-by, big boy!"

I waved back. Oh, this had been clever of me. Now I was out of here!

Baby told me that I would have to do whatever she said. She told me to lie down. She took off my shoes.

"I want to go downstairs and sit in the lobby, and tonight I want to eat in the dining room," I said, and watched her craftily to see what she'd say now. Now I'd find out whether I was free.

"Of course, we'll eat downstairs if you want to," she said. "But you must always keep your hand on my shoulder in case you get dizzy."

For Baby this was one of the most difficult decisions to make. She feared that I was too weak to eat in the hotel dining room. On the other hand, it was more important than anything else to free me of my delusions and to prove to me that we could act as free individuals. Yes, I felt so dizzy that everything started revolving if only I lifted my head. But I was going to walk straight anyhow. I wanted to put on my shoes myself, but they didn't fit any more. Baby said, "The left one goes on the left foot and the right one on the right foot." How could she see that?

It was difficult to walk straight. Baby was right, I held on to her shoulder. Why eat? How clumsy these eating utensils were!

"Watch me, how I do it," she said. I watched carefully to see how she used her knife and fork. Crazy! My gums hurt.

There was much confusion in the streets—people, vehicles, people, noise, noise. . . .

I wanted to go to bed.

"My gums hurt very much, really, Baby, look!"

My mouth was scalded by the hot soup. What is hot? What is cold? What is sweet? What is sour? Why does the water steam?

Oh, it was all so difficult. My feet didn't touch the ground. I was suspended in the air and I felt so dizzy. I was dizzy for a long, long time.

After a while Tony came with a big, comfortable car.

"Hello, Rudi," he said. "Now we're going to Terre Haute. I'm taking you to my little country place, Lingen Lodge. You can stay there—the longer the better, and there you can sit by the lake and fish."

A large park—almost a real woods—an artificial lake, and on its border a charming little house with all imaginable comforts. A turquoise swimming pool, a huge terrace. It was so quiet there. Only at night you could hear strange animal noises. It sounded eerie. The great, reddish moon—bigger than any moon I ever saw—hung low in the sky. Its golden light fell on the pale yellow, fragrant water lilies that half-choked the lake with their enormous leaves.

The nights were as hot as the days. On the bed the contours of my body were outlined in sweat. It was the humid heat of Indiana that does such wonderful things for the Indiana corn.

During the afternoons Mary and Tony Hulman came to see us, almost every day, if only for a little while. They brought fresh-roasted coffee and ate the Swedish cakes Baby baked. They filled the deep freeze with food of all kinds. They took more care of us than any one in this world ever had.

In 1946, the fact that the entire industry had been geared

for years to supplying the army was still noticeable. Household goods were available only in a limited number. Meat was scarce, bacon almost impossible to get. Two pairs of nylon stockings for the women, and only in the shops where one was registered. Tony got everything. He brought bacon and steaks and coffee. He brought us the mail and took Baby's letters with him, and in those days she wrote a great deal. For two months she slept only fitfully. Later she told me I had walked around so much at night she'd been afraid I'd fall into the swimming pool. Toward four in the morning we'd drink a bottle of ginger ale and then, for a few hours, we slept.

27

Gradually I became a human being again. The routine of daily life became a matter of fact once more. It is easy to relearn something one has already known.

I was beginning to long for home. In Lugano I would find the old Rudi again.

Mary and Tony Hulman, Wilbur Shaw and his wife escorted us to Chicago and took us to the plane. Tony had two little packages, one for me, one for Baby.

"Don't open till you're up in the air," he said.

Baby stood by the door of the plane till the last minute, waving and smiling. Parting was difficult. It was farewell to so many things—both dreadful and beautiful, to so many people we had come to love, to Mary and Tony Hulman whose kindness and friendship were so great that they had lightened even the darkest days.

Fastened in my seat, I opened the package: a golden cigarette lighter, "From Mary and Tony to Rudi." For Baby the same in a smaller size.

Home was lovely, but still I found no rest. The ground beneath my feet was still a cloud that kept evaporating under my weight. What was the use of living now? Why didn't I die over there? I had already experienced a kind of death. I had gone—and now I was back again. Now I must die once more. Why did God let me live? What did He have in store for me?

When I could drive again I began to gather new courage. I tested myself with great severity. Nothing had changed. I drove exactly as before. Behind the steering wheel I was almost happy again.

Only after I had spent several months in Sweden with Baby did my head begin to clear, and then I discovered the ground under my feet again. The bracing air of the sea and the woods had permeated my being.

In November, in Tessin, in Bellinzona, I became a Swiss citizen. I'd been at home there for twenty years, whenever my nomadic life gave me a few weeks' or days' time. I had left Berlin in 1929.

During the winter, when we were in Zurich, I went to the Mercedes garage to pick up my toolbox that had remained in the transport crate of the car. I didn't get it. I never got it back. They had registered it as German property at the property control office. For over twenty years Walz had worked on my racing cars with those tools.

The existence of the two marvelous little racing cars had aroused the desire of ownership among many racing drivers and automobile engineers. Rumors were flying around. They spoke of an English offer—a buyer willing to pay 220,000 Swiss francs for both cars; the permission of the Bank of England was supposedly available.

America, too, was greatly interested in the cars. I believe that all interested parties overlooked the fact that, although the cars were magnificent indeed, without well-trained racing drivers, and lacking the enormous staff of technicians, mechanics and material they could never be used satisfactorily.

I had to do something to prevent the sale of the cars which were supposed to belong to me.

In view of the claims I had against the firm of Mercedes since they had blocked my pension in April 1942, I could legally attach the cars.

In 1948 I had to sue the property control office for release of the cars. Dr. Haspel was a witness in the Zurich court. He tried, in all candor, to explain the circumstances that had existed, when a written agreement would have been disastrous at that time. Our firm was being watched closely—they even went through the wastepaper baskets.

I won that first round in the battle for the silver arrows. But the Zurich Higher Court won the last one because: ". . . the agreement for the gift of the two automobiles to Caracciola did not constitute a transfer of the property which, under Swiss and German law, is essential to the concept of ownership."

After losing the suit, I was willing to believe that there is no justice in life.

In 1950 an ad appeared in the papers with the offer of the war loot: 2 Mercedes-Benz, 1½-liter racing car, Model 1. . . . Sales terms and details to be obtained from the undersigned. Bids must be received on or before December 15.

The amount of the offered sums were kept secret. The highest offer came from Switzerland, from the now Swiss-owned Mercedes-Benz AG in Zurich. The second highest came from England.

It was consoling to think that the little cars would remain in the family. When I visited the Mercedes Museum last summer I saw that the fought-for silver arrows had returned home. The one that we had fixed up in Zurich for racing was standing there just as if it had never been away on a trip. I should have liked to have attended their triumphant return, because the cars owed it to me that they weren't sent abroad to have their innards torn apart for study.

28

We spent the summer of 1950 in Sweden. In the fall, Dr. Haspel wrote me that as of September there would be practice on the Nuerburgring again. There was a possibility that we might participate in the race in the Argentine with the prewar 3-liter cars. He asked me if I was willing.

Of course I was willing. We were there at the beginning of September. It was raining. My eyes were gladdened by the sight of the country. The restaurant was as cozy as ever and in the evening Neubauer was telling stories, and there were Hermann Lang and his wife Lydia, Fritz Riess and his wife, and a new member of the racing family was practicing along with us: Karl Kling.

We each did three laps. The practice car was hard as a board. Did we really drive in a Grand Prix with this? Twelve years ago? The course was bad and slippery. The slipperiness came from the mossy spots on the course, which had not been in use for so long. They'd had some races, but only sports-car races, and those cars didn't drive in the corners where we drove. I felt suddenly nauseous. I stopped, went away and sat down in our car. What could this mean? Was it the bouncing car or was it—me?

I tried to drive again, then I was sick. It was in plain sight of all. I went upstairs to our hotel room and wished I were dead. Baby came after me.

"Listen, Rudi," she said. "Kling and Lang, they were awfully pale around the gills, too. Lang said, 'I'm not going to drive that heap again; it stinks so much, it makes me ill.' And he hasn't driven it again either."

Yes, I thought, those gasoline fumes were penetrating. I had to talk to Neubauer. They should check the car.

It was indeed a defect in the car. The escaping fumes had made us all sick. Nobody wanted to admit it until they saw me—then they knew. If we all were sick, it must be the fault of the car.

Argentina was not a success. In spite of their annoyance at my unwillingness to drive I was glad I didn't have to race those ancient Grand Prix cars in that tough climate.

Progress was marching with giant steps at Mercedes. Dr. Haspel lived to see only the beginning of a fabulous achievement to which he himself had contributed in such decisive fashion. On January 6, 1952, he died of a stroke after delivering one of his fascinating, humorous speeches at a dinner for the firm's executives.

Wilhelm Haspel was an ingenious man of many talents. He loved beauty. He appreciated music and rare books. He was an enthusiastic hunter, an excellent amateur photographer, and a great leader of men. All the firm's employees had stood behind him and the worker's council had often come to him to discuss their most burning problems.

He loved his beautiful, elegant wife who managed his home with exquisite taste and care. He loved the good life, the strong cigars, the heady wines. He didn't know the limits of his strength. What he could accomplish in an hour was a full day's task for other men. He kept his hand in everything that happened.

Half a year after his death his wife Bimbo died too. It can be said she died of a broken heart.

"Rudi," she told me when I reached her after Haspel's death, "I should have liked so much to grow old with him."

In the factory that year, under the technical guidance of Fritz Nallinger, Chief Engineer Rudolf Uhlenhaut had built the lightest, most fascinating of all sports cars ever: the 300 SL Mercedes.

The door of the car opened upward, a fact that occasioned much comment. It created a great deal of trouble in sports-car races because the racing authorities refused to recognize this peculiar entry as having a door, according to strict rules. I think it was again our Neubauer who found the right answer:

"Nowhere is it written that a door can open only sideways."

As usual, he won.

In May 1952 we started with these 300 SL sports cars in the Mille Miglia, the 1000-mile race in Italy. I went around the course in my touring car first, then one day I did one lap in spite of the heavy Easter traffic in Italy. The course of the race was directly reverse to what it had been in 1931, but I could remember all the tricky spots.

Baby would say, "We're going to arrive at a railroad crossing now."

I'd look at the hill ahead of us and say, "No, that's not until we get behind that hill, and it's an underpass."

Baby was amazed.

I took that practice lap rather fast even in the touring car. Baby doesn't like fast driving and she kept holding on to things. Even so she took notes about the course, and clocked the time it took us to traverse the cities.

The Mille Miglia race took place in the worst possible weather. It rained before we even started. Hundreds of automobiles were starting with one minute's interval each. Of our team I started first. Then Kling, then Lang. On the wet, slippery road Lang went into a road marker fifty kilometers after the start and could not go on.

On the long stretch before Ancona, on the Adriatic, a Mercedes appeared in my rear-view mirror—Kling. He passed me. I estimated him to be about 15 kilometers faster than I. . . . There are no miracles on the straightaway. Everyone gets what he can out of his car. Weren't our three cars identical?

Kurrle was holding on to the side. He—my co-driver—was so big and strong that he could barely move in our coupé. After Pescara, where the road turns away from the sea and leads across a mountain road to Rome, the motor began to heat up. Kurrle was pointing at the thermometer. I'd already seen it, but I couldn't stop out in nowhere. I had to find a gas station, but one where they had a watering can in sight. Kurrle kept pointing at the thermometer again and again. All right. We stopped. We poured in water and went on. Twice more we were forced to stop for water.

In spite of the loss of time we arrived in Brescia in good shape. Our car came in fourth. Bracco won the race, Kling running second. I wasn't a bit tired. I was wildly happy that, after a twelve-year interval, I could drive a 1,000-mile race without feeling tired.

The car had driven so smoothly. The steering had been gentle and precise. To drive races in such a luxurious sports car was a splendid adventure.

I thought of the jittery, hammering steering wheel of my heavy 2000-kilo Mercedes sports car with which I won the 1000-mile race in 1931, on stony, dusty roads—dear God, what a difference! It was quite plain what progress automobile construction had made since then.

Later I was told that Lang and Kling had been given the two faster, more recent models and that I'd been assigned a

slower and—they figured—more reliable car. I was annoyed.
They should have given me a choice. I felt in such good form
that I'd have insisted on driving the more advanced model with
Lang.

29

Before the 24-hour race in Le Mans, a short sports-car race was to take place in Bern. The practice periods for sports cars were very short—the drivers of Formula I cars got the lion's share of practice, of course. By the time we were ready for the start, time had passed and so we couldn't really take more than two to three laps—much too little time to discover any serious weaknesses.

At the start I got off first—it was almost like in the old days on that beautiful course. I missed only the high singing whine of the supercharged cars of that period.

Daetwyler, the well-known Swiss racing driver, had been the fastest during practice in his 4-liter Ferrari. However, in starting, he seemed to have let in the gear too soon in his excitement —the car said *hup* and stood still.

During the second lap my car began to get restless. Whenever I touched the brakes, it flinched and skidded. Time and again it tried to get away from me. There was something the matter with the brakes. But there was no point in stopping at the pits; the race was too short. I'd rather let my teammates pass me and take it easy. Main thing was to bring the car to the finish line, then we might end up with four Mercedes in the lead.

I drove conservatively but steadily, and braked as little as possible. In the thirteenth round it happened. At about 160 kilometers an hour I came hurtling out of a long serpentine turn and, at the next bend, the car got balky. The left hind wheel was blocked. The brake refused to let go; the brake lining stuck. Stubborn as a tank, the car ran into a tree, although I tried with all my might to defeat its purpose.

The tree crashed with a tremendous impact across the road—the instant of impact of the actual collision has been erased from my memory. I only recall thrusting my left, sound leg against the floor and holding the steering wheel away from me with all my strength to prevent the right hip joint from being crushed again.

The car was a total wreck—poor little car. But Uhlenhaut would be happy to see that his tubular chassis had withstood the impact of the collision. One could not ask for a better proof of its solidity.

When the ambulance men arrived I had recovered consciousness. I could feel it—the left leg was gone. Carefully the men pulled me from the car. They put me on a stretcher mounted to the side of a motorcycle, and drove me through the woods to the Red Cross tent.

Meanwhile five cars had pulled up before the obstacle I'd made for them—the tree. They couldn't drive on until minutes later, after the tree was pulled aside.

My wife was standing in the timekeeper's booth between Forsthaus bend and the stands, behind the sandbags that served as protection against skidding cars. According to her watch I was long overdue. But it didn't always have to be an accident that caused a delay—several other cars were also late. Then she knew, and the mechanics knew, that a crash, or something, must have occurred. No news came for a while. For where she stood she was unable to hear a loudspeaker. Then—as she told me a few weeks later—a man came suddenly running by.

"Terrible, terrible!" he was shouting. "That Caracciola—

fractured skull—leg broken. . . ." And he ran on with his arms in the air.

With those words, all feeling left Baby. She stood as if turned to stone. Then, like an automaton, she took the time chart and the stop watch and walked stumbling along the wood path to the Red Cross tent. Police regulations demanded that accident victims, dead or alive, be brought to the Red Cross tent first.

A man took Baby into his car and gave her a lift to the tent. At exactly the same moment when the men took the stretcher off the motorcycle to carry me inside, she got out of the car. I raised my hand to wave at her so she wouldn't be so alarmed at seeing me all covered with blood. The flesh wound at my chin was bleeding badly. Baby held on to the tent pole while they removed my clothes. The thigh was swollen enormously and hurt like the devil. They gave me a shot, which helped.

In Baby's face I could see only her eyes—everything else was drained of color.

"Rudi—oh, Rudi . . ." was all she could say.

"I'm lucky," I told her. "Thank God it's the left leg that's smashed. Probably it'll be shorter now, and I won't limp any more."

I didn't know that the knee was broken too.

In a racing accident you have no choice of doctors. Races are held on Sundays, and on Sundays doctors are on alternate shifts. It was also customary that victims of racing accidents were brought to the municipal—in this case the Cantonal Hospital. However, my friend Fritz Christen, the Swiss automobile sports president, ordered that I was to be brought to a fine private hospital.

The ambulance then carried me hither and yon, over the bridges that led across the race course. It was a long, complicated road. The matter of the pillows and blankets was complicated too—one set belonged to the race course, and had to remain there. Another set belonged to the ambulance outfit. Then, in the operating room of the hospital, I received the final set belonging to the hospital. When you're in such a painful position, all the blankets in the world are a matter of indifference to you. Others, however, are held responsible for the blankets. . . .

I was put into a traction device—a thirty-pound weight hung from the leg, with an elastic stocking that pressed my toes together so that I still have a crippled small toe. And so I had to lie, motionless, for four months.

People were very good to me. So much kindness was shown me by friends all over the world and even from strangers. My room was filled with flowers. A small refrigerator stood on the balcony, and Baby's table was piled high with letters which she answered for me, working far into the night.

Sometimes I felt I could not lie still another moment. From month to month I hoped for recovery. After four months the doctor removed the traction apparatus, put a crate at the foot of the bed and told me to push against it with my foot, as hard as I could. That hurt terribly. The thigh started to swell. After twenty-four hours the fracture was back where it was along with the pain.

Once more they drove a pin through the knee and once more they hung the weights from the leg. An operation was unavoidable now.

Dr. Gusti Preiss, the famous bone surgeon, was to perform the operation. I had to be moved to Zurich. First, Baby telephoned Director General Wagner of the Daimler-Benz AG to inform him of the new situation. Wagner told my wife to take all steps necessary for my recovery.

"Don't be afraid of expense—the best doctor, the best care for our good old Caracciola. Nothing matters except that we get him restored to good health. We're behind you all the way."

Unfortunately Director Wagner died before we could meet again.

The doctor in charge was annoyed by my decision to be taken to Zurich and by my wife's agreeing to it.

"You alone must bear the responsibility for taking him away from here," he told her.

I saw Baby turning to stone. But she got hold of herself and said, "If a man is in this pitiful condition, I suppose somebody must bear the responsibility for him. I shall bear it."

They had to put me in a plaster cast for the trip. This had to dry for two days. Underneath the plaster I itched as if they'd built in a swarm of fleas.

"Baby, help me. Please scratch under the plaster. I can't stand it any more."

So Baby would take the handle of the fly swatter, insert it between skin and plaster up to the itching areas. It gave me the most marvelous relief I could imagine at the time.

A modern Zurich ambulance, whose driver was a sports enthusiast, took me to Zurich to the Hirslanden clinic.

Gusti Preiss and I liked each other from the first moment. Gusti was and is a passionate sportsman himself—football is his favorite sport.

He operated on the thigh and joined the fracture with a special pin. Before, I had begged him to shorten the ends of the bone so that the longer leg would be as short as the right. He didn't want to take off that much, but it was made a little shorter after all.

Gusti came to see me every day. From the end of the hall we would hear his light step, his voice. I looked forward to seeing him every day. He always had a cheerful word and he was a kind man, who felt genuine compassion toward his patients.

He'd come into the room briskly, "Well, how's the young champion?"

I was as well as anyone could be, lying in bed with a bandaged leg that felt like a log. After four weeks Gusti operated on the broken knee. The knee was a problem. For four months it had been left alone; the fracture had pulled apart and the muscles had retracted. Knee operations are extremely painful and Gusti knew it.

"Yes, yes, my boy. Just another day of patience and then it won't hurt so much any more."

I did not want injections if I could possibly do without them. The next night it was even worse. It was so bad that I folded my hands and prayed to God for help. When Gusti Preiss came, I complained aloud. From then on he called me "the silent sufferer."

For almost five months I lay motionless in the Hirslanden clinic before Gusti put me on my feet alongside the bed. During all these months we had collected a small household in that sickroom.

There was a bird house on the balcony, fastened where I could see the birds that were my guests—Hirslanden is on the edge of a wood—finches, titmice and nuthatches were the hungriest. The star of the show was a woodpecker. He'd hang from the walnut-filled net and whirl around. He wore a little red cap that matched his little red breeches. His wings were speckled black and white. Sometimes he came twice a day and I'd ring for the nurses so that they, too, could watch the performances of that acrobat.

I read mystery stories far into the night while Baby tried to reduce the mountains of letters. It was a hopeless task; daily the letter carrier brought more than she could possibly answer. And crossword puzzles—for the first time I regretted not having been more eager to learn foreign languages in school.

We celebrated Christmas in the clinic, with Christmas tree and candles. A family I'd never known arrived with three children. The little girl wore a white gown covered with golden stars and carried a tiny Christmas tree in her hand. The smallest of the children was as fascinated as I by this Christmas angel. The older boy recited a poem his father had written. In the poem I was the hero and soon, soon, it was hoped "Caratch" would drive in the Bern race again.

Now and then the driver of the ambulance came to see whether I was being taken care of in Zurich better than in Bern. He usually brought consolation in the form of cherry brandy. And flowers—more and more flowers, an ocean of flowers.

Director Wagner had ten bottles of pink champagne delivered and thus we celebrated the New Year, more extravagantly than ever at home. Baby had decorated my bed with paper streamers in all colors. Cheerfully we greeted the arrival of the New Year because the New Year was going to bring me recovery. We toasted the future that would spare us ever from plaster casts and operations!

30

In spite of the special pin the fracture healed very slowly. After the usual procedures—wheel chair, crutches, then canes and thermal baths, the X-ray discovered that the steel pin had become bent inside the bone. Panic. Wheel chair again. . . .

For another two months I sat in my wheel chair at home. As time went on I got to be rather agile with it. I rolled from one room to the other and later from the terrace down the garden path. Baby was going to install a horn in my "one-foot" motor. She was no longer safe from me, I kept popping up wherever she wasn't expecting me.

Just before Easter, Dr. Preiss and Professor Boehler came from Vienna to Lugano for a consultation. Both agreed: the patient should walk. Walking would speed recovery.

Easter became for me a sort of resurrection in more ways than one. On uncertain, clumsy legs I began again to walk with canes.

During the summer we stayed for a few weeks with our friends Ernst Henne and his wife in their lovely, flower-covered country house on Starnberg Lake, surrounded by magnificent old trees and a velvety lawn that stretched all the way to the lake. Here I could almost walk without a cane.

Water and sun, motorboat rides, watching the others swimming and water skiing—by and by the memory of the ordeal faded in those cheerful surroundings.

A year later Gusti Preiss removed the pin and ceremoniously handed it to me as the final trophy of my multifarious career.

All that was five years ago. It would have been terribly hard for me to have to stand aside if Mercedes had continued participating in auto racing.

Now the decisive years have gone by without much pain. Fate has pulled the switch for me.

Sometimes I think back of the great—the greatest—days of auto racing, when in a single race six or seven of the drivers had an even chance of winning.

I've had no other passion in life than to race automobiles, to be the fraction of a second faster than the other fellow. I must, of course, admit that it was never for a minute the thought that this would make me one of the long roster of men who have contributed to making the automobile popular. And yet, without automobile racing the rapid development of the passenger car would have been unthinkable. The harsh demands on material and all parts of the car during a race cannot be replaced altogether by a mechanical testing stand.

Races on the open road will soon end, and that is only right because we are approaching with giant steps a time when such events are no longer feasible with traffic what it is.

People today are inclined to think that automobiles have reached perfection, but technicians and engineers are looking farther into the future, working tirelessly on improving the device that has so profoundly affected human existence.

If I, by my neck-breaking profession and technical experiences gathered in automobile racing, have contributed to making the automobile more reliable and safe, then my life behind the steering wheel has meant more than a mere fight to win.

In spite of many hardships, life has been good to me. Not many children had as carefree and happy a childhood as I in Remagen on the Rhine.

Not many racing drivers have been able to come out alive from smashed heaps of metal, and certainly very few are privileged to work in a profession, from early youth onward, which they love as passionately as I love motor sports.

However where there is sun, there is also shadow. But as the years go by the shadows fade, and only the radiance and the beauty remain.

I no longer drive races, as "to everything there is a season and a time to every purpose under heaven." Life has become quieter, but my little wife is busy packing suitcases again. We're going down to Italy where I'm to demonstrate the latest Mercedes 300 SL—because I am still driving for the three-pointed star.

Epilogue

The Rudolf Caracciola story would by no means be complete without mention of the years following his retirement from competition, that twilight period intervening between recovery from his severe accident in Berne in 1952 and his unexpected, untimely death in 1959. In this connection, it was typical of this great sportsman that he approached the Finish Line of Life with the same determination and courage that had characterized his racing career.

In the early fall of 1955, responding to a proposal from Daimler-Benz, Rudi Caracciola undertook a leading role in a special sales program aimed at the thousands of American and British NATO troops stationed in Europe. This market, while potentially important for the German export drive, was nevertheless hard to get at and difficult to exploit. The widely dispersed troops, the language difficulties, unavailability of suitable dealers and demonstration cars, and even military regulations themselves, all added to the obstacles involved. With his typical energy, thoroughness, enthusiasm and great personal charm Rudolf Caracciola organized and led a campaign of shows and demonstrations which toured military installations from Tripoli to Oslo, from Austria to Scotland. His fame preceded him and it is small wonder that air base commanders suspended flying to enable high speed demonstrations on the runways; that officers' and NCO's and service clubs vied with each other to entertain the former champion and see actual films of his most thrilling victories; and that even the busiest generals found time to receive the quiet man with the grey hair, sparkling smile and painful limp, in order to talk of the past and often as not to take a fast spin in the Mercedes-Benz 300 SL.

For four full and busy years this goodwill and demonstration program sparked the military sales throughout Europe and contributed in no small measure to the record-breaking Mercedes-Benz sales of these years. In 1959 it was even planned to expand this highly productive and successful activity to the Far East, but Fate decided otherwise.

From the year's beginning, the champion had not been well. Various examinations failed to disclose a cause, and so, putting aside all personal comfort and well-being, Rudolf Caracciola toured the U.S. Air Force bases in England during April and May. Significantly, he remarked to some of his many friends there that perhaps he wouldn't be alive for a tour in the following year. In June the British forces stationed in Northern Germany were visited and Rudolf, as usual, was accorded a hero's welcome. Shortly afterward a severe case of yellow jaundice brought home the seriousness of his illness, which in spite of treatment continued to worsen. Admission to a leading hospital in Germany followed where a diagnosis of advanced liver cirrhosis was made. The end was soon at hand; the Great Race was over; the victor in more than 100 major Grand Prix events and the holder of untold motoring accolades had taken the Checkered Flag for the last time.

Perhaps Fate had been kind in that he was permitted an active life to the very end. Certainly the last years had done much to satisfy his strong desire to serve and to be useful, as well as to widen his already tremendous following of friends and acquaintances the world over. That his popularity and esteem remained undiminished by the interval following his retirement from competition was proven at his death, and is to this day still borne out by the respects being paid at the flower-bedecked grave on the heights of Lugano.

ALLAN H. ZANE, JR.
Daimler-Benz, Stuttgart, Germany

Rudolf Caracciola's
Racing Record

Date		Event	Vehicle	Position
1922				
		Round Cologne Run. All-round winner.	M/cycle NSU 7 h.p.	1
June	1	Avus Race, Berlin.	Fafnir 6 h.p.	4
July	2	Opel Track Race.	Fafnir 6 h.p.	1
1923				
April	3	Stadium Race, Berlin. Best time of the day.	Ego 4 h.p.	1
		Rastatt-Ettlingen. Flat Race. Touring-Cars 6 h.p. 4,5 km. in 2.52 min. = 94,2 km. h.	Mercedes 6/25/40 h.p.	2
July	10–15	Baden-Baden Car Tournament. All-round winner.	Mercedes 6/25/40 h.p.	1
July	19–21	ADAC Tournament Runs. Münnerstadt Hill Climb. Touring Cars 6 h.p. Best time of the day.	Mercedes 6/25/40 h.p.	1
		Pforzheim Hill Climb. Best time of the day.	Mercedes 6/25/40 h.p.	1
		Solitude Hill Climb. Best time of the day. 6 km. in 4.17,3 min. = 83,9 km. h.	Mercedes 6/25/40 h.p.	1
		Best of all touring cars and all automobiles.	Mercedes 6/25/40 h.p.	1
Aug.	18	Silesian Mountain Tournament. All-round winner.	Mercedes 6/25/40 h.p.	1
		Silesian Flat Race.	Mercedes 6/25/40 h.p.	1
		Silesian Hill Climb.	Mercedes 6/25/40 h.p.	1
Sept.	7	Pöhlberg Race. Best time of the day. Winner of the 6 h.p. class.	Mercedes 6/25/40 h.p. Mercedes 6/25/40 h.p.	1 1

Date		Event	Vehicle	Position
Oct.	14	Krähberg Hill Climb, Record. All-round winner, 3,8 km. in 4.08,2 min. = 55,1 km. h.	Mercedes 6/25/40 h.p.	1
		Best time of all automobiles.	Mercedes 6/25/40 h.p.	1
1924				
April	20	Königsaal-Jiloviste Hill Climb. 5,6 km. in 3.57,6 min. = 84,5 km. h. All-round winner. New track record in 3.57,6 min.	Mercedes 1,500 c.c. S	1
		Winner of class touring cars under 1,750 c.c.	Mercedes 1,500 c.c. S	1
May	18	Hercules Hill Climb. 4,5 km. in 4.11,4 min. = 64,5 km. h. Best time of touring cars.	Mercedes 1,500 c.c. S	1
		Winner of class 3 category.	Mercedes 1,500 c.c. S	1
May	25	Teutoburgerwald Race. 31 km. in 18.17,6 min. = 101 km. h. All-round winner. Winner of cars category until 10 h.p. Best time of the day.	Mercedes 1,500 c.c. S	1
		Winner of the Nikolaus Dürrkopp Challenge.	Mercedes 1,500 c.c. S	1
May	30	Silesia run at Zittau, hill climb. Best time of all motor-cycles.	M/cycle Garelli 350 c.c.	1
		Silesia run at Zittau, hill climb. Best time of the day, in 5.49 min.	Mercedes 1,500 c.c. S	1
		Silesia run at Zittau, flat race.	M/cycle Garelli 350 c.c.	1
		Silesia run at Zittau, flat race. 4 km. in 2.25,2 min. = 99,2 km. h. Best time of the day. Challenge trophy for fastest time.	Mercedes 1,500 c.c. S	1
		Lückendorf Pass Hill Climb. 4 km. in 3.23,8 min. = 70,7 km. h.	Mercedes 1,500 c.c. S	1
June	22	Gottleuba Hill Climb. 5,5 km. in 3.45,1 min. = 87,9 km. h.	Mercedes 1,500 c.c. S	1
June	29	Black Forest Hill Climb. Best time of sports cars.	Mercedes 1,500 c.c. S	1
July	(?)	Kupferhammer-Huckenfeld Hill Climb. 3,1 km. in 3.10,4 min = 58,6 km. h. Winner of category.	Mercedes 1,500 c.c. S	1
July	9	Automobile Tournament at Baden-Baden. Rastatt-Durlach Flat Race, 5 km. in 2.22,1 min. = 126,5 km. h.	Mercedes 1,500 c.c. S	1

Date		Event	Vehicle	Position
July	19	Eifel Circuit at Nideggen. Racing cars, 10 laps each. 33 km. in 5.27,50 h. = 60,4 km. h. Best time of the day.	Mercedes 1,500 c.c. S	1
July	28	Silesian Mountain Run. 300 km. for cars 6 h.p. Best time of the day.	Mercedes 1,500 c.c. S	1
		"Sieben Kurfürsten" Hill Climb.	Mercedes 1,500 c.c. S	1
		Reichensteiner Kamm Hill Climb.	Mercedes 1,500 c.c. S	1
		Reichenstein-Kamenz Flat Race. Fastest time of the day. Outright winner of the run.	Mercedes 1,500 c.c. S Mercedes 1,500 c.c. S	1 1
Aug. 16–17		Klausen Pass Hill Climb, Switzerland. Sports car. 21,5 km. in 20.29,2 min. = 63 km. h.	Mercedes 1,500 c.c. S	1
		Klausen Pass Hill Climb. Touring car. Record of turing cars.	Mercedes 1,500 c.c. S	1
		Flying kilometer on the Urnerboden. 1 km. flying start in 29 sec. = 124,2 km. h. Outright winner.	Mercedes 1,500 c.c. S	1
Aug. 10–19		ADAC Tournament Run. 1800 km. All-round winner.	Mercedes 1,500 c.c. S	1
		"Hohe Sonne" Hill Climb at Eisenach in 2.40,2 min. Best time of all automobiles.	Mercedes 1,500 c.c. S	1
		Kriescht Flat Race. 6 km. in 3.24,3 min. = 105,7 km. h. Best time of all automobiles.	Mercedes 1,500 c.c. S	1
1925				
June	17	Teutoburgerwald Race. 85 km. in 45.17,2 min. = 112,6 km. h. Best time of the day. New track record.	Mercedes 4 cyl. 2000 c.c. S Typ Targa Florio	1
June	28	Hercules Hill Climb at Kassel. 4,5 km. in 4.49,3 min. = 56 km. h. Best time of all racing cars.	Mercedes 1,500 c.c. S	1
July	17–24	Robert-Batschari Run and Baden-Baden Tournament. All-round winner.	Mercedes 6 litre 6 cylinder touring car 24/100/140 h.p.	1
July	19	Forstenrieder Park Flat Race, Munich. 10 km. in 4,59 min. = 120,4 km. h. Best time of all cars.	Mercedes 24/100/140 h.p.	1

Date		Event	Vehicle	Position
July	23	Flat race on the road, Hügelsheim-Rastatt. 4 km. in 2.05 min. = 115,2 km. h.	Mercedes 24/100/140 h.p.	1
		Aptitude Tournament.	Mercedes 24/100/140 h.p.	1
July	24	Kniebis Hill Climb at Freudenstadt. 6 km. in 6.07,8 min. = 58,7 km. h. Best time of touring cars. Best time of all cars in the three speed competitions.	Mercedes 24/100/140 h.p.	1
		Winner of the Robert-Batschari Challenge.		
		Winner of the team prize of the Automobile Club of Württemberg. (Caracciola, Neubauer, Sailer) Trophy of honor for excellency in the special performances.	Mercedes 24/100/140 h.p.	1
Aug.	15	Hill climb and flat race at Freiburg. 1 flying kilometer in 26,5 sec. = 135,5 km. h.	Mercedes 24/100/140 h.p.	1
Aug.	16	ADAC Mountain Record Run at Schauinsland, Freiburg. 12 km. in 12.15,2 min. = 58,7 km. h. Best time of touring cars.	Mercedes 24/100/140 h.p.	1
Aug.	23	Klausenpass Hill Climb. 21,5 km. in 19.38,40 min. = 60,1 km. h.	Mercedes 24/100/140 h.p.	1
		Winner of the category 5000 c.c. Team prize with Christian Werner and Otto Merz.	Mercedes 24/100/140 h.p.	1
1926				
March	16	Teutoburgerwald Race. Class over 12 h.p. 51 km. (three laps) in 34.45,2 min. = 88 km. h.	Mercedes 24/100/140 h.p.	1
May	30	Hercules Race Hill Climb. Sports cars. 4,5 km. in 4.17 min. = 63 km. h.	Mercedes 24/100/140 h.p.	1
June	9–13	Baden-Baden Automobile Tournament. Ettlingen-Rastatt Flat Race. 4,9 km. in 2.07,2 min. = 138,7 km. h. Best time of all cars.	Mercedes 24/100/140 h.p.	1
		Kniebis Hill Climb. 6 km. in 6.28,8 min. = 55,5 km. h. Best time of sports cars.	Mercedes 24/100/140 h.p.	1
		Kniebis Hill Climb. Best time of touring cars.	Mercedes 24/100/140 h.p.	1

Date		Event	Vehicle	Position
June	26	South German Rally. 3500 km. no penalty. All-round winner in sports car.	Mercedes 24/100/140 h.p.	1
		24-hour race in the Taunus. No penalty, all-round winner in sports car.	Mercedes 24/100/140 h.p.	1
		Technical performance trial run at the Solitude (Stuttgart).	Mercedes 24/100/140 h.p.	1
July	11	Grand Prix of Germany at Avus track, Berlin. 392,3 km. in 2.54.17,8 hours = 135,2 km. h. Trophy for the fastest lap.	Mercedes 8 cyl. 2,000 c.c.K	1
July	22	Grand Prix of Europe and Grand Prix of Guipuzcoa. 12 hour race for touring cars = 1057,1 km. = 101,6 km. h. with driving mechanic H. Kühnle. Winner was Otto Merz & W. Gärtner Mercedes. 1069 km. = 101,8 km. h.	Mercedes 24/100/140 h.p.	2
July	31	International record runs at Freiburg. Kilometer record Oberrimsingen at Breisach. 1 km. flying start with 1,3 km. in 23,4 sec. = 153,7 km. h. Record for sports cars.	Mercedes K 2,000 c.c., 6 cyl. 24/110/160 h.p.	1
Aug.	7–8	Klausen Pass Hill Climb. 21 km. in 20.50,2 min. = 61,9 km. h. Best time of touring cars. Record.	Mercedes K 24/110/ 160 h.p.	1
		Klausen Pass Race, the flying kilometer on the Urnerboden. 1 km. in 23,4 sec. = 153,7 km. h. Best time of touring cars.	Mercedes K 24/110/ 160 h.p.	1
Aug.	22	Kipsdorf-Oberbärenburg-Altenberg Hill Climb Race. 5 km. in 3.32,2 min. = 84,8 km. h. Best time of the race and the day.	Mercedes K 24/110/ 160 h.p.	1
Sept.	12	International Hill Climb Race at Semmering (Austria). 10 km. in 8.02,1 min. = 74,7 km. h. Best time of touring cars. Record. Grand Mountain Prize of Austria for touring cars.	Mercedes K 24/110/ 160 h.p.	1

Date		Event	Vehicle	Position
Sept.	12	International Hill Climb Race at Semmering (Austria). 10 km. in 6.40,8 min. = 89,9 km. h. Best time of the day. Record. Definitive winner of the challenge cup for automobiles.	Mercedes racing car Model K 4500 c.c.	1
1927				
June	19	Inauguration race on the Nürburgring, Eifel, Germany, for sports cars. 359,6 km. = 12 laps in 3.33.21 hours = 101,1 km. h. Best time of the day.	Mercedes-Benz S—6800 c.c.K. 6 cyl. 26/120/ 180 h.p.	1
June	23–30	Kartell race of the Automobile Club of Germany. 2700 km. No penalty. Silver trophy, medal and trophy for outstanding merit.	Mercedes-Benz 2000 c.c. 8/38	1
July	5–9	Automobile Tournament at Baden-Baden. Ettlingen-Rastatt Flat Race. Sports car. 4,9 km. in 1.46,4 min. = 165,8 km. h. Best time of the day.	Mercedes-Benz S	1
July	9	Hill climb race for sports cars. 11,8 km. in 8.00 min. = 88,5 km. h. Best time of sports cars. Trophy for outstanding performance.	Mercedes-Benz S	1
		Aptitude test.	Mercedes-Benz S	1
		All-round winner of tournament at Baden-Baden.	Mercedes-Benz S	1
Aug.	6–7	International record days at Freiburg. International Kilometer flat race. 1 km. and 1,4 km. starting distance in 21,2 sec. = 170,1 km. h.	Mercedes-Benz S	3
		International mountain record race on the Schauinsland, Freiburg. 12 km. in 10.23 min. = 69,3 km. h. Best time of the sports cars. Record.	Mercedes-Benz S	1
Aug.	13	Klausen Pass Hill Climb Race. National Race. 21 km. in 17.43,8 min. = 72,3 km. h. Class record for touring cars.	Mercedes-Benz S	1

Date		Event	Vehicle	Position
Aug.	14	International Race at the Klausen Pass. 21,5 km. in 17.35,4 min. = 73,3 km. h. Best time of the sports cars. New Klausen record for sports cars.	Mercedes-Benz S	1
Sept.	(?)	Dreiecks-Rennen at Bukow, Germany, for sports cars. 124 km. in 1.18.15,6 hours = 95 km. h. Best time of the day. Trophy of President Hindenburg.	Mercedes-Benz S	1
Sept.	18	Kilometer race at Oostmalle at Antwerp, Belgium. Sports car. 1 km. in 18,5 sec. = 194,6 km. h. Best time of the day.	Mercedes-Benz S	1
Sept.	25	Teutoburgerwald Race at Bielefeld. 51 km. in 26,11 min. = 116,9 km. h. Best time of the day. Fastest lap.	Racing car type Targa Florio Mercedes-Benz 2,000 c.c.	1
1928				
June July	27– 1	Automobile Tournament at Baden-Baden. Flat Race. 5 km. in 1.49,4 min. = 164,5 km. h. Best time of sports cars.	Mercedes-Benz SS 6,800 c.c. 6 cyl. K 27/160/ 200 h.p.	1
		Hill Climb Race. 10 km. in 7.43,8 min. = 77,6 km. h. Best time of sports cars.	Mercedes-Benz SS	1
		Aptitude test.	Mercedes-Benz SS	1
		All-round winner of the tournament. Winner of the Batschari challenge.	Mercedes-Benz SS	1
July	15	Grand Prix of Germany on the Nürburgring. Sports car with Christian Werner. 509,4 km. in 4.54.24,4 hours = 103,9 km. h. average. Fastest lap Caracciola 111,6 km. h. Erna Merck memorial trophy for the fastest German car.	Mercedes-Benz SS K 6800 c.c. 6 cyl. 27/170/225 h.p.	1
July	29	Gabelbach Hill Climb Race. Racing car. 4 km. in 2.11,8 min. = 73 km. h. Best time of racing cars. Best time of day.	Mercedes-Benz SSK	1
Aug.	5	International ADAC Race. Mountain record race on the Schauinsland at Freiburg. 12 km. in 9.51,4 min. = 73 km. h. Best time of racing cars. Best time of day.	Mercedes-Benz SSK	1

Date		Event	Vehicle	Position
Aug.	12	Ratisbona Hill Climb Race. Racing car. 4 km. in 2.33,6 min. = 93,7 km. h. Best time of day. Record.	Mercedes-Benz SSK	1
Aug.	26	Col des Montes, hill climb race at Chamonix, France. 4 km. in 2.33,6 min. = 93,7 km. h. Best time of day. Record of track. Best time of racing cars.	Mercedes-Benz SSK	1
Sept.	10	Salzberg Hill Climb Race. Racing car. 3,5 km. in 3.37,2 min. = 58,1 km. h. Winner in category. Special trophy for outstanding performance and sporting spirit.	Mercedes-Benz SSK	1
Sept.	16	Semmering Hill Climb Race. Racing car. 10 km. in 6.40,3 min. = 89,9 km. h. Best time of the day. New Semmering record.	Mercedes-Benz SSK	1
Sept.	29	Kilometer race at Oostmalle, Antwerp, Belgium. 1 km. in 18,5 sec. = 194,6 km. h. New Belgian racing car record.	Mercedes-Benz SSK	1
1929				
April	16	Grand Prix of Monaco, Monte-Carlo. Racing cars. 100 laps = 318 km. in 3.58.33,6 hours = 79,9 km. h.	Mercedes-Benz SSK	3
April	28	International Hill Climb Race. Zbraslav-Jiloviste, Czechoslovakia. 5,6 km. in 2.49,2 min. = 119,1 km. h. Best time of racing cars. Record.	Mercedes-Benz SSK	1
June	7–9	Hannover Automobile Tournament in Bad Pyrmont. Flat race, racing car.	Mercedes-Benz SSK	1
		Hill climb race. Racing car. 4,3 km. in 3.10,8 min. = 81,1 km. h. Best time of the day. Record.	Mercedes-Benz SSK	1
June	19–23	Automobile Tournament in Baden-Bad·· Flat race. 5 km. in 1.43,1 min. = 174,1 km. h. Best time of racing cars. Record.	Mercedes-Benz SSK	1

Date	Event	Vehicle	Position
	Hill climb race up to Bühlerhöhe. Racing car. 10 km. in 7.09,3 min. = 83,8 km. h. Best time of the day. New track record.	Mercedes-Benz SSK	1
Aug. 7–12	International Alpine Trial. 2600 km. Trophy cup of the Alps.	Mercedes-Benz type "Nürburg"	1
Aug. 17	International Tourist Trophy, Belfast, Ireland. 410 miles in 5.37,40 h. = 117,2 km. h. Best time of the day. Fastest lap. New track record.	Mercedes-Benz SSK	1
Aug. 19–24	International Automobile Week, St. Moritz, Switzerland. Bernina flat race. Racing car. 1 km. back and forth in 20,4 sec. = 176,5 km. h.	Mercedes-Benz SSK	1
Sept. 29	ADAC long distance race on the Nürburgring for touring cars without supercharger. 8 hours.	Mercedes-Benz "Nürburg"	1
	Also team prize: Caracciola, Merz, Werner.	Mercedes-Benz "Nürburg"	
1930			
Jan. 29	Monte-Carlo Rally. Reval to Monte-Carlo.	Mercedes-Benz "Nürburg"	
April 12–13	1000 Mile Race (Mille Miglia), of Brescia, Italy. 17.20.17,4 hours = 92,8 km. h. Victory of the category with Caracciola-Werner.	Mercedes-Benz SSK	1
May 11	Zbraslav-Jiloviste Hill Climb Race in Czechoslovakia for the European Mountain Championship. 5,6 km. in 2.52,7 min. = 116,7 km. h. Best time of day. Record.	Mercedes-Benz SSK	1
June 29	Collo Della Maddalena Hill Climb Race at Cuneo, Italy, for the European Mountain Championship. 66,5 km. in 41.24,2 min. = 96,4 km. h. Best time of sports cars. Record.	Mercedes-Benz SSK	1
July 12	Shelsley-Walsh Hill Climb Race, England, for the European Mountain Championship. 1000 yards in 46,8 sec. = 70,3 km. h. Best time of sports cars. Record.	Mercedes-Benz SSK	1

Date		*Event*	*Vehicle*	*Position*
July	18–19	Grand Prix of Ireland in Dublin. Handicap race. 70 laps = 300 miles in 3.28,24 hours = 139 km. h. All-round winner. Winner of the Irish *Times* Trophy, the Eirann-Cup of Campbell and the Irish Independence Cup.	Mercedes-Benz SSK	1
Aug.	10	International Klausen Pass Hill Climb Race. 21 km. in 17.04,6 min. = 75,5 km. h. Record for sports cars.	Mercedes-Benz SSK	1
Aug.	17	ADAC mountain record on the Schauinsland, Freiburg, for the European Mountain Championship. 12 km. in 9.38 min. = 74,7 km. h. Best time of sports cars. Record.	Mercedes-Benz SSK	1
Aug.	24	Mont-Ventoux Hill Climb Race, France, for the European Mountain Championship. 21,6 km. in 15,2 min. = 86 km. h. Best time of the day.	Mercedes-Benz SSK	1
Sept.	8	Grand Prix of Monza, Italy. 1 heat: 14 laps = 100,8 km. in 39.49,4 min. = 151,8 km. h. Sports car.	Mercedes-Benz SSK	2
Sept.	14	Semmering Hill Climb Race. 10 km. in 6.35,4 min. = 90,9 km. Best time of sports cars. Record.	Mercedes-Benz SSK	1
Oct.	5	Hohnstein Hill Climb Race. All-round winner.	Mercedes-Benz SSK	1
Sept.	21	Schwabenberg Hill Climb Race, for the European Mountain Championship. 4,64 km. in 3.21,1 min. = 83,1 km. h. Best time of the day. New Record.		
		European Mountain Championship, 1930.	Mercedes-Benz SSKL (6 cyl.–300 h.p.)	1
1931				
April	12–13	1000 Mile Race (Mille Miglia), Brescia, Italy, with mechanic Wilhelm Sebastian. 1635 km. in 16.10.10 hours = 101,1 km. h. Record. Daimler-Benz received a gold medal from the King of Italy and a trophy of the Automobile Club of Germany.	Mercedes-Benz SSKL	1

Date		Event	Vehicle	Posi-tion
May	17	Rabassada Hill Climb Race, Spain, for the European Mountain Championship. 4,9 km. in 3.45,4 min. = 78,2 km. h. Best time of all cars. All-round winner. Record.	Mercedes-Benz SSKL	1
May	31	Zbraslav-Jiloviste, Czechoslo-vakia Hill Climb Race for the European Mountain Cham-pionship. Sports cars up to 8 liter. 5,6 km. in 2.42,7 min. = 123,9 km. h. All-round win-ner. Best time of day. New track record.	Mercedes-Benz SSKL	1
June	7	Eifel race at Nürburgring. 312 km. = 40 laps in 2.50.47,2 hours = 109,6 km. h. Best time of the day.	Mercedes-Benz SSKL	1
June	14	Kesselberg Hill Climb Race for the European Mountain Championship. 5 km. in 4.03,4 min. = 73,8 km. h. Best time of sports cars.	Mercedes-Benz SSKL	1
July	19	Grand Prix of Germany on the Nürburgring. 501,8 km. = 22 laps in 4.38,10 hours = 108,03 km. h. All-round win-ner. Record.	Mercedes-Benz SSKL	1
July	26	ADAC mountain record run on the Schauinsland, at Frei-burg. 12 km. in 8.51,2 min. = 81,3 km. h.	Mercedes-Benz SSKL	1
Aug.	2	Avus Race, Berlin. 294,4 km. = 15 laps in 1.35.07,6 hours = 185,7 km. h. Best time of the day. Fastest lap.	Mercedes-Benz SSKL	1
Aug.	16	Tatra Hill Climb Race, Po-land, for the European Moun-tain Championship. 7,5 km. in 2.45,7 min. = 81,9 km. h. All-round winner. Best time of the day. New sports car record.	Mercedes-Benz SSKL	1
Aug.	30	Mont-Ventoux Hill Climb Race for the European Moun-tain Championship. 21,6 km. in 15.22 min. = 84,4 km. h. All-round winner. Best time of the day. New track record.	Mercedes-Benz SSKL	1

Date		Event	Vehicle	Posi-tion
Sept.	20	Drei-Hotter Hill Climb Race, Hungary, for the European Mountain Championship. 4 km. in 2.44,8 min. = 87,4 km. h. European Mountain Championship, 1931.	Mercedes-Benz SSKL	1
1932				
April	17	Grand Prix of Monaco, Monte-Carlo. 100 laps = 318 km. in 3.32.28 hours.	Alfa-Romeo Monoposto (2600 c.c.)	2
May	22	Avus Race, Berlin.	Alfa-Romeo Monoposto	2
May	30	Eifel Race, Nürburgring. 319 km. in 2.48.22 hours = 113,780 km. h. New record and fastest lap in 11.42,4/5 min. Best time of the day.	Alfa-Romeo Monoposto	1
		Grand Prix of Italy, Monza.	Alfa-Romeo Monoposto	3
		Kesselberg Hill Climb Race for the European Mountain Championship. New racing car record. New track record.	Alfa-Romeo Monoposto	1
June	19	Grand Prix of Lemberg, Poland. 66 laps = 200 km., average 86 km. h. Fastest lap average 89 km. h. New record.	Alfa-Romeo Monoposto	1
July	4	Grand Prix of France, Reims 5 hour race.	Alfa-Romeo Monoposto	3
July	16	Grand Prix of Germany, Nürburgring. 25 laps of 22,810 km. = 570,250 km. in 4.47.22,8 hours = average 119,3 km. h.	Alfa-Romeo Monoposto	1
July	24	Gaisberg, Hill Climb Race for the European Mountain Championship. 12 km. in 7.57,08 min. = 89,811 km. h. Fastest time of the day.	Alfa-Romeo Monoposto racing car	1
Aug.	7	Klausen Pass Hill Climb Race for the European Mountain Championship. 21 km. in 15.50 min. = 81,470 km. h. New class record. Best time of all racing cars. Best time of all automobiles and new Klausen Pass record.	Alfa-Romeo Monoposto racing car	1

Date	Event	Vehicle	Position
	ADAC mountain record race at Schauinsland, Freiburg, for the European Mountain Championship. 12 km. in 8.35,8 min. = 83,75 km. h. New absolute track record.	Alfa-Romeo Monoposto racing car	1
Sept. 4	Mont Ventoux Hill Climb Race, for the European Mountain Championship. 23 km. in 15.12,4 min. = 86,220 km. h. New absolute track record.	Alfa-Romeo Monoposto racing car	1
Sept. 11	Grand Prix of Italy, at Monza. 1 heat in 33.24 1/5 min. = 179,620 km. h. Fastest lap. Average = 181,086 km. h.	Alfa-Romeo Monoposto racing car	1
	Finale: 1 in 1.07.15 hour = 178,402 km. h.	Alfa-Romeo Monoposto racing car	1
	Coppa Acerbo, at Pescara, Italy.	Alfa-Romeo Monoposto racing car	2
	Stelvio, Italy, Hill Climb Race.	Alfa-Romeo Monoposto racing car	3
	Monte Cenisio, Italy, Hill Climb Race.	Alfa-Romeo Monoposto racing car	3
	European Mountain Championship, 1932. International Championship of the Alps for 1932.		
1933	Caracciola suffered an accident during training in Monte-Carlo in 1933 and was out of racing the entire year. It was not until August 1934 that he was able to race again.		
1934	(*An asterisk indicates 750 kg. racing car formula*)		
Aug. 5	International Klausen Pass Hill Climb Race. 21,5 km. in 15.22,1 min. = 84,7 km. h. Best time of the day. New record.	Mercedes-Benz racing car 750 kg.—Grand Prix-Formula. 8 cylinder, above 2 litres	1
Aug. 19	Mountain Grand Prix of Germany at Freiburg. 12 km. in 8.32,6 min. = 84,3 km. h.	Mercedes-Benz*	2
Sept. 9	Grand Prix of Italy, at Monza. 116 laps = 501 km. in 4.45,47 hours = 105,2 km. h. with Luigi Fagioli. Best time of the day.	Mercedes-Benz*	1
Sept. 23	Grand Prix of Spain, San Sebastian. 30 laps = 519,5 km. in 3.20.24 hours = 155,5 km. h.	Mercedes-Benz*	2

Date	Event	Vehicle	Posi-tion

Speed records on the record track at Gyon, Hungary.

Oct. 28–30   Racing cars class C (3–5 litres)
1 km. flying start in 11,34 sec. = 317,5 km. h.
1 mile flying start in 18,3 sec. = 316,6 km. h.
International record class 3–5 litres:
1 mile standing start in 30,71 sec. = 188,6 km. h. World Record.
Speed records at the Avus, Berlin, racing car class C (3–5 litres)
5 km. flying start in 57,69 sec. = 311,98 km. h. International
Class Record. New track record of the Avus = 4.43,9 min.

1935

May 12	Grand Prix of Tripoli, North Africa. 524 km. in 2.38.47,6 hours = 198 km. h. New track record.	Mercedes-Benz*	1
May 26	International Avus race, Berlin. 2 heat: 97,9 km. in 24,27 min. = 240,03 km. h.	Mercedes-Benz*	1
June 16	International Eifel race at Adenau, Nürburgring. 11 laps = 250,9 km. in 2.08.02,6 hours = 117,8 km. h. Best time.	Mercedes-Benz*	1
June 23	Grand Prix of France, at Montlhéry. 40 laps = 500 km. in 4.00.54,6 hours = 124,6 km. h.	Mercedes-Benz*	1
June 30	Grand Prix of Spain, at Barcelona. 70 laps = 265 km. in 2.28.28 hours = 107,2 km. h.	Mercedes-Benz*	2
July 14	Grand Prix of Belgium, at Spa. 34 laps = 506,6 km. in 3.12.31 hours = 157,5 km. h. Trophy of the King of Belgium. Belgian racing car record.	Mercedes-Benz*	1
July 28	Grand Prix of Germany, at Nürburgring. 22 laps = 501,8 km. in 4.11.32 hours = 119,9 km. h.	Mercedes-Benz*	3
Aug. 25	Grand Prix of Switzerland, at Berne. 70 laps = 509,6 km. h. in 3.31.12,2 hours = 144,3 km. h. New track record.	Mercedes-Benz*	1
Sept. 22	Grand Prix of Spain, at San Sebastian. 519 km. in 3.09.59 hours = 164 km. h. New track record.	Mercedes-Benz*	1
	European Champion for racing cars 1935. Champion of Germany 1935.		

Date		Event	Vehicle	Position
1936				
April	13	Grand Prix of Monaco, Monte Carlo. 100 laps = 318 km. in 3.49.20,4 hours = 83,2 km. h.	Mercedes-Benz*	1
May	10	Grand Prix of Tripoli, North Africa. 40 laps = 524 km. in 2.34.56,4 hours = 202,9 km. h.	Mercedes-Benz*	4
May	17	Grand Prix of Tunis, Tunisia, North Africa. 30 laps = 381,42 km. in 2.22.44,6 hours = 160,3 km. h.	Mercedes-Benz*	1
June	7	Grand Prix of Spain, at Barcelona. 80 laps = 303,5 km. in 2.42.13 hours = 111,6 km. h.	Mercedes-Benz*	2
July	26	Grand Prix of Germany, at Nürburgring. 22 laps = 501,8 km. with Luigi Fagioli.	Mercedes-Benz*	5
Oct.	26	Record trial runs on the Frankfurt-Heidelberg Autobahn. International records class B, racing cars 5–8 litres. 1 km. flying start in 9,88 sec. = 364,4 km. h. 1 mile flying start in 15,79 sec. = 366,9 km. h. 5 km. flying start in 52,86 sec. = 340,5 km. h.		
Nov.	11	Record trial runs on the Frankfurt-Darmstadt Autobahn. International records of class B, racing cars 5–8 litres. 5 miles flying start in 1.26 min. = 336,8 km. h. 10 km. flying start in 1.48,47 min. = 331,9 km. h. *World Record* 10 miles flying start in 2.53,73 min. = 333,5 km. h.		
1937				
May	9	Grand Prix of Tripoli, North Africa. 40 laps = 524 km.	Mercedes-Benz*	6
May	30	International Avus race, Berlin. 1 heat, 7 laps = 135,5 km. in 32.29,6 min. = 250,4 km. h.	Mercedes-Benz*	1
June	13	International Eifel race at Nürburgring. 10 laps = 228,1 km. in 1.43.01,4 hours = 133 km. h.	Mercedes-Benz*	2
July	25	Grand Prix of Germany, at Nürburgring. 22 laps = 501,8 km. in 3.46.00 hours = 133,2 km. h. New track record.	Mercedes-Benz*	1
Aug.	1	Mountain Grand Prix of Germany at Schauinsland, Freiburg. 12 km. in 8.17,7 min. = 86,9 km. h.	Mercedes-Benz*	3

Date		Event	Vehicle	Position
Aug.	8	Grand Prix of Monaco, Monte-Carlo. 100 laps = 318 km. in 3.08.48 hours = 101,1 km. h. Fastest lap of the race.	Mercedes-Benz*	2
Aug.	22	Grand Prix of Switzerland, at Berne. 50 laps = 364 km. in 2.17.39,3 hours = 158,6 km. h.	Mercedes-Benz*	1
Sept.	12	Grand Prix of Italy, at Leghorn. 50 laps = 360,9 km. in 2.44.54,4 hours = 131,3 km. h. New track record. Trophy of the King of Italy and Trophy Ciano.	Mercedes-Benz*	1
Sept.	26	Grand Prix Masaryk, at Brünn, Czechoslovakia. 15 laps = 437,1 km. in 3.09.25,3 hours = 138,4 km. h. New track record. New lap record.	Mercedes-Benz*	1
Oct.	2	Grand Prix at Donington, England. 80 laps = 250 miles in 3.01.40 hours = 132,9 km. h.	Mercedes-Benz*	2
		Coppa Acerbo race, Pescara, Italy.	Mercedes-Benz*	5
		European Champion for Racing Cars 1937.		
		Champion of Germany 1937.		
1938				
		Record trials on the Frankfort-Darmstadt Autobahn.		
Jan.	28	International records class B racing cars (5–8 litres) 1 km. flying start in 8,32 sec. = 432,7 km. h. 1 mile flying start in 13,40 sec. = 432,7 km. h.		
April	10	Grand Prix of Pau, France. 276,9 km. in 3.10.50 hours = 87,1 km. h. Fastest lap.	Mercedes-Benz 3,000 cc Grand Prix formula	2
May	15	Grand Prix of Tripoli, North Africa. 25 laps = 524 km.	Mercedes-Benz 3,000 cc	3
July	3	Grand Prix of France, at Montlhéry. 500 km. in 3.06.19,6 hours = 161,3 km. h.	Mercedes-Benz 3,000 cc	2
July	24	Grand Prix of Germany, at Nürburgring. With Hermann Lang. 22 laps = 510,8 km.	Mercedes-Benz 3,000 cc	2

Date		Event	Vehicle	Position
Aug.	14	Coppa Acerbo, at Pescara, Italy. 16 laps = 412,8 km. in 3.03.45,5 hours = 134,8 km. h.	Mercedes-Benz 3,000 cc	1
Aug.	21	Grand Prix of Switzerland, at Berne. 50 laps = 364 km. in 2.32.07,8 hours = 143,6 km. h. Best time on the track. Best lap time.	Mercedes-Benz 3,000 cc	1
Sept.	11	Grand Prix of Italy, at Monza. 60 laps = 419,6 km. in 2.42.39,4 hours = 146,7 km. h. v. Brauchitsch drove 3 laps.	Mercedes-Benz 3,000 cc	3

European Champion for Racing Cars 1938.
Golden Medal of the AIACR for Outstanding Performances.

1939

Record runs on the Dessau Autobahn.

Date		Event	Vehicle	Position
Feb.	8	International records in the racing-car class D (2–3 litres) 1 km. standing start in 20,56 sec. = 175,1 km. h. 1 mile standing start in 28,32 sec. = 204,6 km. h.		
Feb.	9	1 km. flying start in 9,04 sec. = 398,2 km. h. 1 mile flying start in 14,50 sec. = 399,6 km. h.		
Feb.	14	1 km. standing start in 20,29 sec. = 177,4 km. h.		
May	7	Grand Prix of Tripoli, North Africa. 30 laps = 393 km. Double victory with Hermann Lang.	Mercedes-Benz 1500 cc with supercharger	2
May	21	International Eifel race at Nürburgring. 10 laps = 228,1 km.	Mercedes-Benz 3,000 cc	3
July	23	Grand Prix of Germany at Nürburgring. 22 laps = 501,8 km. in 4.08.41,8 hours = 121,9 km. h. Best time on the track. Best lap time.	Mercedes-Benz 3,000 cc	1
Aug.	20	Grand Prix of Switzerland, at Berne. 1 heat 20 laps = 145,6 km.	Mercedes-Benz 3,000 cc	2
		Finale: 30 laps = 218,4 km. Fastest lap.	Mercedes-Benz 3,000 cc	2

Champion of Germany 1939.

Summary of Rudolf Caracciola's Records and Championships

149 first places
20 second places
12 third places
5 4–6 places

1930	European Mountain Championship	Mercedes-Benz SSK sports car
1931	European Mountain Championship	Mercedes-Benz SSKL sports car
1932	European Mountain Championship International Championship of the Alps	Alfa-Romeo Monoposto racing car 2600 c.c.
1935	European Champion	Mercedes-Benz 750 kg. racing car
1937	European Champion	Mercedes-Benz 750 kg. racing car
1938	European Champion and Golden Medal of the AIACR	Mercedes-Benz 750 kg. racing car
1935	Champion of Germany	Mercedes-Benz 750 kg. racing car
1937	Champion of Germany	Mercedes-Benz 750 kg. racing car
1939	Champion of Germany	Mercedes-Benz 3000 c.c. racing car
1934	2 International records at Gyon	Mercedes-Benz 3–5 l racing car class C
	1 Worlds record at Gyon	Mercedes-Benz 3–5 l racing car class C
	1 International record class 3–5 litre at Avus	Mercedes-Benz racing car C
1936	3 International records Frankfurt-Heidelberg Autobahn	Mercedes-Benz 5–8 litre racing car B
	2 International records Frankfurt-Darmstadt Autobahn 1 World record	Mercedes-Benz 5–8 litre racing car B
1938	2 International records Frankfurt-Darmstadt Autobahn (432,7 km. h.)	Mercedes-Benz 5–8 l racing car B
1939	5 International records at Dessau (399,6 km. h.)	Mercedes-Benz 2–3 l racing car D